# LEWANDOWSKI

LEWANDOWSKI

MATT AND TOM OLDFIELD

ULTIMATE
FOOTBALL HEROES

# LEWANDOWSKI

## FROM THE PLAYGROUND
## TO THE PITCH

DINO

First published by Dino Books in 2021,
an imprint of Bonnier Books UK,
The Plaza, 535 King's Road, London SW10 0SZ
Owned by Bonnier Books,
Sveavägen 56, Stockholm, Sweden

🐦 @dinobooks
🐦 @footieheroesbks
www.heroesfootball.com
www.bonnierbooks.co.uk

Text © Matt Oldfield 2021
The right of Matt Oldfield to be identified as the author of this work has been
asserted by him in accordance with the Copyright, Designs and Patents Act 1988.

Design by www.envydesign.co.uk

Paperback ISBN: 978 178946 453 5
E-book ISBN: 978 178946 454 2

British Library cataloguing-in-publication data:
A catalogue record for this book is available from the British Library.

Printed and bound in Great Britain by Clays Ltd, Elcograf S.p.A.

1 3 5 7 9 10 8 6 4 2

FSC
MIX
Paper from
responsible sources
FSC® C018072
www.fsc.org

*For Noah and Nico,*
*Southampton's future strikeforce.*

ULTIMATE
FOOTBALL HEROES

Matt Oldfield is an accomplished writer and the editor-in-chief
of football review site Of Pitch & Page. Tom Oldfield is a
freelance sports writer and the author of biographies on
Cristiano Ronaldo, Arsène Wenger and Rafael Nadal.

Cover illustration by Dan Leydon.
To learn more about Dan visit danleydon.com
To purchase his artwork visit etsy.com/shop/footynews
Or just follow him on Twitter @danleydon

# TABLE OF CONTENTS

# ACKNOWLEDGEMENTS

First of all, I'd like to thank everyone at Bonnier Books UK for supporting me throughout and for running the ever-expanding UFH ship so smoothly. Writing stories for the next generation of football fans is both an honour and a pleasure. Thanks also to my agent, Nick Walters, for helping to keep my dream job going, year after year.

Next up, an extra big cheer for all the teachers, booksellers and librarians who have championed these books, and, of course, for the readers. The success of this series is truly down to you.

Okay, onto friends and family. I wouldn't be writing this series if it wasn't for my brother Tom. I owe him so much and I'm very grateful for his belief in me as an author. I'm also very grateful to the rest of my family, especially Mel, Noah, Nico, and of course Mum and Dad. To my parents, I owe my biggest passions: football and books. They're a real inspiration for everything I do.

Pang, Will, Mills, Doug, Naomi, John, Charlie, Sam, Katy, Ben, Karen, Ana (and anyone else I forgot) – thanks for all the love and laughs, but sorry, no I won't be getting 'a real job' anytime soon!

And finally, I couldn't have done any of this without Iona's encouragement and understanding. Much love to you.

## CHAPTER 1

# JOINING FOOTBALL'S TOP TABLE

*17 December 2020*

Robert paced from one side of the room to the other and could feel sweat trickling down the side of his cheek. Taking a deep breath, he wiped his cheek with the back of his hand. 'There's no reason to be nervous,' he told himself.

But, as much as he was a cool and calm finisher on the pitch, Robert always felt butterflies in his stomach on award nights. Plus, this was no ordinary awards night. Tonight, he was a finalist for FIFA Men's Player of the Year award, alongside Lionel Messi and Cristiano Ronaldo.

He caught a glimpse of himself in the hallway mirror and grinned. He had to admit – he looked good. His wife, Anna, had patiently helped him choose the perfect suit for this special occasion and it looked even better now than when he had first tried it on.

Just then, Robert's phone pinged twice. He walked over and scooped it up off the table. Due to health concerns, FIFA had decided to cancel the in-person awards show this year in favour of a video event – and these latest texts were from his FIFA representative, confirming that it would be another thirty minutes before he was added to the video call.

Robert sat down on the sofa and called Anna. 'Is it almost showtime?' she asked.

'Not quite,' he replied, laughing. 'But they've given me some amazing snacks while I wait.'

'Well, you can use the time to practise your speech. They say singing is a good way to warm up your voice!'

'No chance!' Robert replied, grinning. But he was feeling better now. Anna always knew how to calm him down.

As he caught up on her news and the latest updates from their daughters, the thirty minutes flew by. His phone buzzed with a new call from his FIFA representative, who had one quick message. 'Stand by – the TV crew want you on screen in two minutes.'

Robert had walked through the plan countless times with the FIFA team, yet he still felt a little shaky as he sat down in front of the camera, checked his microphone, and adjusted his earpiece. Thirty seconds and counting.

'It's time for the final award of the night,' the presenter explained. 'Over to you, Gianni.'

FIFA President Gianni Infantino appeared on the screen, walking down a hallway and clutching the trophy. He would be hand-delivering it to one of the three finalists for FIFA Men's Player of the Year – Messi, Ronaldo and Lewandowski. All three players were now on camera in the top part of the screen.

'And the winner is…' Gianni paused to build up the tension, then entered the room where Robert was sitting. '…Robert Lewandowski!'

Robert smiled as Gianni passed him the trophy. It

was heavier than he expected and looked a bit like the World Cup trophy. 'Thank you,' he said. 'This is a real honour.'

Then he turned to face the camera, just like he had been told during the rehearsal. 'I am very proud to have won this award. It was a team performance really and it was really impressive what we were able to win together. It's an incredible feeling and a privilege to be a finalist with Leo and Cristiano.'

Robert smiled as the voice in his earpiece told him he had another twenty seconds to wrap up his speech. 'This is a night that I will never forget. Thank you.'

As the presenters delivered their final words of the night, Robert's phone buzzed. 'That's a wrap. You're free to go.'

He let out a big breath and started to take off his bow tie. The messages from friends and family were now pouring in, congratulating him on his award. Anna sent a string of emojis – two hearts, a thumbs up and a trophy – from their daughter, Klara. 'She says "tell Daddy he was great",' Anna wrote.

Then came what felt like the hundredth FIFA text

of the night. 'One last thing – can you sign back into the event for a few more minutes?'

Even though he was eager to get home to his family, Robert did as he was told. The screen popped open again and he had to blink twice to believe his eyes. His childhood idol, Thierry Henry, was staring back at him. 'Whoaaaaa!'

'Congratulations!' Thierry said, laughing at Robert's shocked face. 'You deserve it. You were outstanding and you've been outstanding for a long time. It takes something special to finish ahead of Leo and Cristiano – and you did it.'

Robert was speechless. 'Thank you,' he finally managed to reply. 'This means so much to me.'

What a night, and what a season. Robert had fired Bayern Munich to an unstoppable Champions League-Bundesliga-German Cup Treble, scoring a sensational fifty-five goals along the way, and this major individual honour was the icing on the cake. This year, he had risen to the top table of world football, and tonight he had confirmed it.

As he chatted to Thierry, Robert saw his whole

career flash before his eyes. The boy who was once called 'too skinny' and 'too weak' now had more trophies than he could have ever dreamed of. There had been plenty of difficult moments along the way when Robert could have simply walked away, but he refused to give up.

With the shiny trophy tucked under his arm, Robert knew he was now being rewarded for overcoming those obstacles. He reflected once again on how proud he was to have done it the hard way.

## CHAPTER 2

# SURROUNDED BY SPORT

As little Robert wrapped himself in his towel and darted towards his bedroom, he slipped across the floor and almost bumped into the wall.

His mother, Iwona, appeared in the doorway. 'How many times have I told you to dry your feet on the mat?!' she complained.

Robert knew better than to try to answer that question. 'Sorry, Mum!'

Iwona smiled. It was hard to be angry with her son when she had been just the same at his age – full of energy, fearless. And she knew why Robert was rushing, too. Sure enough, a few minutes later, she heard her son dribbling a ball around in his bedroom.

'What's all that noise?' Robert's dad, Krzysztof, asked as he came up the stairs.

'Last week, I told Robert that he could only play with that little ball in his room if he'd had his bath and was in his pyjamas before seven. Since then, I don't think I've ever seen anyone get ready quicker.'

Krzysztof laughed. 'That's our son! With our genes, he was never likely to be an artist or musician.'

The Lewandowskis had sport in their DNA. 'We're a family of athletes,' Iwona liked to say. She had been a professional volleyball player, and Krzysztof had played judo and football.

Krzysztof went to check on Robert and tell his son that he would be turning off the light in five minutes. 'I used to have a ball just like that,' he said, pointing to the black-and-white ball that Robert was kicking against the wall, where two shoes were acting as goalposts.

As Robert carried on playing, Krzysztof added: 'I'd play for hours in my room in the winter and then in our back garden the rest of the year. That's when I first started to love the game. I joined a team with my friends, then the local youth team…'

Krzysztof stopped and looked up. Robert had stopped playing with the ball and was now sitting on the edge of his bed. 'Keep going, Dad. Tell me more. I know you and Mum are really good at sport, but I've never heard the stories about how you became so good.'

'Well, get into bed first,' Krzysztof said, pulling a small chair across the room and perching on the edge. Iwona poked her head round the door and Krzysztof signalled for her to join them. She sat down on the end of the bed.

'Robert was just asking about the secret to sporting success,' Krzysztof explained.

Iwona smiled. 'Ah, you mean our family secret. Well, that's a long story. I'm not sure we've got time for that tonight.'

'Please!' Robert pleaded, sitting up in bed and putting on his most angelic face. 'I'll go straight to sleep after.'

'Okay,' began Krzysztof, 'the first thing you need to know is that you cannot get anywhere without hard work. When I first started playing volleyball, I would practise with my team every Wednesday, then on Mondays and Fridays I'd wake up at 6am to do extra running before school.'

'Really?'

Krzysztof chuckled at the confusion on Robert's face. His son liked his sleep.

'Yes,' Iwona continued. 'You have to be willing to be the first to arrive for training and the last to leave. You have to listen to your coaches and work on the things they suggest. And then you need a little bit of luck, of course.'

Her path to becoming a professional volleyball player had not been easy, and she was determined to make sure Robert understood that there could be no shortcuts.

'You have to make sacrifices too,' Krzysztof added.

'What does that mean?' Robert asked. He was wide awake now and trying to memorise all this good advice.

'Well, when you get older, there will be lots of other things you want to do – like going out with your friends, eating junk food, or staying up late.

To become a football player or a volleyball player, sometimes you miss out on those moments.'

'But there's one secret ingredient to always remember,' Iwona said, leaning forward to kiss her son on the forehead. 'You have to believe in yourself, no matter what, because every player in every sport has difficult times. By getting through those, you can really enjoy the good times.'

As Krzysztof got up to follow Iwona out of the room, he turned to Robert. 'And don't forget,' he whispered. 'Football and judo are much better than volleyball.'

'I heard that!' Iwona replied, pretending to kick Krzysztof in the shin.

Robert giggled and snuggled under his blanket. Having two parents who played sport at a high level must give him a head-start in following in their footsteps, he thought. But before he could start following all of his parents' advice, he needed to decide which sport was right for him.

As his eyelids got heavier and heavier, Robert drifted off to sleep and dreamt about winning his first trophy.

## CHAPTER 3

# CHOOSING FOOTBALL

Iwona clapped her hands impatiently and tried to get everyone into position for the photo. It was Robert's sixth birthday and she was determined to have at least one good photo to put in her album. The day had been a blur, with Robert opening his presents early in the morning and bouncing around the house even before the two slices of birthday cake in the afternoon. His younger sister, Milena, had spent at least an hour outside in the back garden with him, reluctantly agreeing to be a goalkeeper just this one time.

'Krzysztof, move a little to the right and put your arm on Robert's shoulder,' Iwona called, as she adjusted the camera. 'Milena, stay where you are and

I'll go next to you.'

She pressed a button and ran round to join them. 'Everyone smile!'

'Wait!' Robert called out suddenly. He jumped up and ran to his room as his parents looked at each other with confused faces. He reappeared seconds later with a football tucked under his arm.

'Seriously?!' Iwona asked, half glaring, half laughing.

Robert winked and got back into position next to his dad. 'Okay. Take two.'

Iwona was already back at the camera, setting up the angle again. 'More like Take 200!'

With the photo finally taken, Robert dribbled the ball into the hallway and practised flicking it from his foot, onto his knee and then up to his chest, before dropping it back at his feet again. The players always made it look easier on TV, he thought, as the ball bounced off his foot and rolled away.

Krzysztof watched from the doorway. He and Iwona had given Robert a chance to try all kinds of sports, but the boy had a clear favourite now.

When Robert stopped to catch his breath, Krzysztof

brought him a cup of water. 'Nice work!'

'Thanks, Dad. But I've got to work even harder if I'm going to become a great striker.'

'Well, don't forget you're still a kid!'

'Do you think I should stop playing some of the other sports and focus on football?' Robert asked suddenly. 'Maybe I'd get better even faster.'

Krzysztof grinned. Clearly, his son was a boy in a hurry! 'Son, when you think about the main skills that a striker needs, what comes to mind?'

Robert thought for a minute. 'Shooting?'

'Sure. Goalscorers have to be good at that. But they also need to have good balance and be agile enough to make good runs. They have to be strong to hold off defenders, and good at jumping too.'

Robert nodded, listening carefully.

'I know you probably think that your gymnastics, judo and volleyball are taking time away from football, but we think it's the opposite. Without even knowing it, you're adding skills that other players don't have.'

'Wow, I didn't think of it like that,' Robert said. 'I'm definitely better at jumping since I started volleyball training.'

'Exactly, and gymnastics is great for your balance and flexibility, which could be huge for avoiding injuries. All I'm saying is don't be in a rush to drop those other sports. At the same time, we want you to be happy. If you're serious about becoming a professional footballer, you'll have to put your full focus on that at some point – and if you really think that time is now, we'll support you.'

Robert smiled. He knew how lucky he was to have his parents 100 per cent behind him. 'Thanks, Dad. Becoming a footballer is what I dream about, but I think I'll keep going with all the sports for now and wait until next year to make a decision.'

In the meantime, it was clear to Krzysztof that Robert had outgrown the kickabouts with his friends in the park. He was ready for tougher challenges, even if that meant playing against older boys. Krzysztof began to make calls to the local team, Partyzant Leszno.

## CHAPTER 4

# LEARNING IN
# LESZNO

As Krzysztof turned off the main road, past the fire station and into the car park, Robert sat up straight in his seat and smiled. He had walked past the Partyzant Leszno pitch so many times over the years, but this morning felt different. It was like he was seeing it all for the first time again – the red sign on the wall, and the yellow club crest with its black-and-yellow ball.

'It all feels real now, doesn't it?' Krzysztof said, as if reading his son's mind. 'But just go out there and do your best. Remember, you wouldn't be wearing that kit if they didn't think you were ready.'

Robert grinned as confidently as he could, while feeling his stomach doing backflips. There had been no pressure during his first two training sessions with the Partyzant Leszno youth team, but today was a proper match against one of the club's older age groups.

'Most importantly, have fun!' Krzysztof called as Robert hoisted his bag over his shoulder and walked over to where his new teammates were waiting. As he watched his son give high fives to two of the boys he knew from school, Krzysztof realised he was as nervous as Robert probably was. But why? Robert was only six, after all. This match was hardly going to make or break his career.

By the time the Partyzant Leszno coaches handed out a few footballs and got the boys passing in small circles, Robert was feeling better. His first touch was sharp and the nerves had been replaced by excitement. Even the biggest Partyzant Leszno supporter would have admitted that the pitch had seen better days, and Krzysztof was reminded of why, as a long pass caught one of the uneven patches and spun away from Robert as he tried to control it. Still, on that morning, Robert thought it was the most perfect pitch in the whole world.

One of the coaches appeared with a small notepad and huddled the boys together to read out the team. 'The strikers will be Robert and Eryk,' he said. 'Take turns dropping back to look for short passes, but make sure one of you is always ready for the long ball.'

Robert tried to look serious and just nod his head, but a big smile quickly spread across his face. He was the new boy and had expected to be on the bench for this first game. But clearly his dad had been right – he must have really impressed the coaches in training.

After a few quick stretches, Robert jogged over to the touchline to get his water bottle. He had been given the Partyzant Leszno shorts and socks last week, but the shirts were always given out on the day of the game.

'Robert, do you want 9 or 10?' Eryk shouted.

With his head still spinning from the team news, it took Robert a minute to understand the question. 'Either shirt number is fine with me, but 9 would be my first choice.'

'Number 9 it is,' Eryk replied, bringing that shirt to Robert and patting him on the shoulder. 'Let's go and score some goals.'

But that would be a difficult task against the older Partyzant Leszno team who were all taller and stronger. As Robert waited for the referee to blow his whistle, he looked over to the touchline and gave a thumbs up to his dad, who gave one back.

It took just ten minutes for Robert to see that he would not win many headers or tackles against boys who were a few years older than him. All he seemed to be doing was chasing defenders. Eryk was having the same problem.

When the ball flew out for a throw-in, Robert called Eryk over to talk about a Plan B. 'We've hardly had a touch so far. We've got to keep the ball on the ground and use our speed.'

Eryk nodded. 'I'm going to drop back to help the midfield. If I get the ball, make the run through the middle and I'll try to find you.'

Eryk's first couple of attempts were easily intercepted, but the third time he chipped the perfect pass over the head of the last defender. Robert got to the ball in a flash, took two touches to set up an easier angle, and then fired a low shot into the bottom corner.

*Goooooooooooooooooooaaaaaaaaaaaaaaaaalllllllllllllll llllllllllll!!!!!!!!!!!!!!!!!!!!*

Robert leapt in the air. A goal with his first shot! Eryk was the first to sprint over and hug him. 'I knew you'd only need one chance to make them pay.'

That afternoon, it was a short-lived lead for the younger Partyzant Leszno boys. The match ended in a 4–1 loss, but Robert would never forget that feeling of seeing the ball hit the back of the net. He talked non-stop on the drive home, with Krzysztof only able to add his opinion on the game when Robert stopped to breathe.

Then Robert told the stories all over again to Iwona and Milena. 'I wish you could have seen it,' he said. 'I hit the shot right into the corner, just like I always practise.'

As Robert climbed into bed that night, he was far too tired for a story. He drifted off to sleep with his dreams already turning to Partyzant Leszno's next game and how he would follow up his debut goal.

## CHAPTER 5

# VICTORIES WITH VARSOVIA

Iwona and Krzysztof had talked about Robert and his football dream every night that week and, finally, they had reached a decision. Next season, Robert would start playing for Varsovia Warsaw to test himself at a higher level. After a whirlwind first year with Partyzant Leszno, even his own coaches admitted that Robert should.

With Robert's age group not available at Legia Warsaw, Krzysztof had contacted Varsovia, and after watching one of the Partyzant Leszno games, Varsovia needed no convincing. Robert had scored four goals that day and set up two more. 'Your son has a unique eye for goal for someone his age,' the Varsovia scout had told Krzysztof and Iwona. 'His instincts, his technique, his movement – it's all very advanced. We'd love to bring him to Varsovia.'

Now Robert was getting the quick tour of the Varsovia training set-up. 'We hope one day that we can re-do the changing room and improve the pitches,' explained one of the Varsovia coaches. 'But, for now, this is where the magic happens.'

Robert shrugged and smiled. 'It looks good to me – I just need goalposts and a ball,' he said. 'That's all that matters.'

'Spoken like a true striker!' the coach replied, smiling.

After the tour, Krzysztof and Robert were led to a small room in the main training ground building, where bottles of water and some snacks were laid out on a table. Before long, they heard the sound of laughter in the corridor and a cheery man strolled into the room. 'Welcome to Varsovia, I'm Marek Siwecki,' he said. 'I'll be Robert's coach this year.'

Robert gave a shy smile as he shook hands. Marek explained more about the type of football he wanted the team to play, and the commitment expected from all the boys, from arriving on time to following instructions. But Robert could see straightaway that Marek had a fun side too, with lots of jokes in their whirlwind twenty minutes together.

This was the beginning of a special bond between Robert and Varsovia which taught him many lessons and shaped the rest of his career. But it came with some big sacrifices, both for him and for the family. With three training sessions per week plus a game at the weekend, Robert was either at school or on the football pitch. There wasn't much time for anything else.

For Krzysztof and Iwona, it was a two-hour drive to get Robert to training – and sometimes even further for his games. 'I know it sounds like a lot,' Krzysztof would tell his friends. 'But it's all worth it to see the joy on Robert's face when he's got the ball at his feet.'

Robert's teammates quickly became important friends. At the end of one training session, Robert was joking with Casimir, who they called Caz, and Florian, who they called Flo. 'You need a nickname,' Flo said, chipping the ball towards his kitbag. Robert shrugged.

'I'm always just Robert,' he replied. 'Though my

dad told me that in England Robert is often shortened to Bob. Sometimes he'll call me that just to make me laugh.'

Caz and Flo looked at each other. 'That's it!' they said at once. Before long, all the boys were calling him 'Bobek' (Little Bob) and, with his skinny frame, the nickname stuck.

As Robert progressed through the age groups at Varsovia, he moved up to work with Coach Sikorski, who helped him to take the next steps as a striker. His shooting was already so good, but he soon learned there was a lot more to the position, including holding the ball up when he had his back to goal and moving without the ball to create space.

After the first few practices, Coach Sikorski called Marek to double-check that the little boy they called 'Bobek', with the skinny legs and the shy smile, was really the one he was so excited about. 'Just wait,' Marek replied. 'Get him in a real game and you'll see what he can do.'

Sure enough, Robert's natural instincts were clear once the season started. Despite being smaller than most defenders, he was fearless when battling for the ball and ruthless whenever he had a chance in the penalty area. Before long, Coach Sikorski and Marek were on the phone every week to discuss Robert's latest performance and how they could keep pushing him to strive for more.

As for Robert, he was just happy to be playing football four times a week. What could be better than that?

## CHAPTER 6

# AN ASSIST FROM THE PRIEST

The morning of his communion service, Robert laid out two sets of clothes – his shirt and trousers for the service and his football kit for a game later in the afternoon. His dad had been very clear that he would need to change in the car if they were going to make it in time for kick-off.

There was no chance of skipping the service. Robert didn't even raise the question. All of his family were planning to be there, and he had put hours into completing the communion classes. Though, as he buttoned up his shirt, he wondered for a second if he should put his kit on underneath. He decided that might get him in trouble if the priest found out.

At the church, Robert spotted some of the other boys from his class. 'Can I sit with them?' he asked his parents.

Krzysztof nodded, putting his jacket down on another pew to save seats for himself and Iwona. 'I'll be right back,' he told Iwona.

Iwona watched in surprise as Krzysztof walked to the front of the church and shook hands with the priest. Leszno was a small place, but it was unusual for them to have a conversation at church before a service.

But Krzysztof had a plan. 'Sorry to ask, but what's the order of the communion service today?' he asked the priest. 'My son, Robert, has a game this afternoon. Any chance he could be one of the first names called?'

The priest grinned. His nephew went to the same school and he knew all about Robert's football dreams. They had even been to watch a few of his games at Leszno.

'I'll see what I can do,' he said, with a wink. 'Tell Robert I expect him to score at least two today!'

Sure enough, Robert was the fourth name to be called up, as the priest moved swiftly through the service. As soon as it was safe to do so, Krzysztof signalled for Robert to quietly slip away to the back of the church. After a quick hug to congratulate him on his first communion, he said: 'Okay, let's go!'

They jogged to the car. As Krzysztof turned onto the motorway, Robert was already wriggling into his kit in the back. 'Dad, how did you persuade the priest to make me one of the first names? I was expecting it to be alphabetical order.'

'Well, it turns out he's a football fan. Once he knew you had a game this afternoon, he wanted to help.'

'Wow, I guess you're right about people in Leszno always wanting to help each other.'

'There's one catch, though. He expects you to score two goals.'

Robert laughed. 'Easy.'

They made it to the pitch with ten minutes to spare. 'I'll bring your bag and water bottle,' Krzysztof said. 'Just run over so they know you're here.'

'We were getting worried!' one of the coaches called out, as Robert sprinted across the pitch and managed to squeeze in a few passes before kick-off.

'He thinks he's too good to warm up, lads,' joked Aleks, his usual strike partner. Robert did a few extra stretches whenever the ball went out for a throw-in, just to prove him wrong.

As he always did, Robert took the first few minutes to assess the defenders he was facing. Were they quick? How tightly were they marking him? Would he win many headers against them? That afternoon, he didn't see many weaknesses – and that usually meant that his movement would have to make all the difference.

Robert dropped deeper to get involved in the build-up play, laying one pass back into midfield and another out to the right wing. But he really came alive in the penalty area. When Aleks dribbled past one defender, he looked up and saw Robert making a quick diagonal run behind the defence. He slid the pass through, and Robert did the rest, firing a shot into the top corner.

*Gooooooooooooooooooooaaaaaaaaaaaaaaaaalllllllllllllll llllllllllll!!!!!!!!!!!!!!!!!!!*

Aleks raced over and jumped on Robert's back. 'I think you ripped a hole in the net with that one!'

Robert grinned as he ran back to the halfway line.
That was exactly the kind of move he was picturing.
The defenders were just as fast as him, but clever
movement always seemed to get him an extra yard.

That first goal opened the game up and soon he and
Aleks were passing their way through on goal again.
This time, Robert cut the ball back and Aleks side-
footed a first-time shot through the goalkeeper's legs.
'I owed you that pass after you set up my goal,' Robert
said, high-fiving his friend.

There was even time in the second half for Robert
to deliver on the priest's request for two goals. A quick
counter-attack finished with a chipped cross to the
back post where he was totally unmarked. He placed
a perfect header just out of the keeper's reach.

*Goooooooooooooooooooooaaaaaaaaaaaaaaaaalllllllllllllll
llllllllllll!!!!!!!!!!!!!!!!!!!*

'Okay, maybe you really don't need to warm up
with us anymore!' Aleks said, as they walked off
the pitch together at the end.

Krzysztof was grinning too. 'You two are
unstoppable,' he said. 'That team will be having

nightmares about you for weeks.'

Robert could hardly believe everything he had done in the space of a few hours. As he climbed into the car and looked forward to a well-deserved nap on the way home, he realised he owed an assist to the priest too.

## CHAPTER 7

# INSPIRED BY THIERRY

As a young striker, Robert tried to learn as much as he could from watching the world's best players on TV. For a few years, Roberto Baggio was his hero, then it was another Italian, Alessandro Del Piero. He loved how easy they made everything look, without ever being the biggest or strongest players on the pitch. Some of his friends were drawn to powerhouses like Christian Vieri and Oliver Bierhoff, but that wasn't his style of play.

But, as Del Piero's career came to an end, Robert was on the lookout for a new idol – and he found one during the 2003–04 season while staying over at his friend Niko's house. Niko's dad was a big

Liverpool fan, and that meant the boys were lounging on the sofa with him on an April afternoon to watch Liverpool play Arsenal.

Robert knew the big names on both teams, but only occasionally saw Premier League games. As Niko and his dad argued playfully about whether Michael Owen or Steven Gerrard was Liverpool's most important player, Robert was drawn to the silky skills of Arsenal's Thierry Henry. Every time Henry got the ball in the Liverpool half, Robert felt himself sit forward on the sofa and hold his breath. It always seemed like something explosive was about to happen.

Niko and his dad were soon high-fiving when Liverpool took the lead. Robert clapped to be polite, but deep down he found himself cheering for Arsenal. He wriggled on the sofa again as Henry sprinted onto a chipped pass, then put his hands over his mouth to hide his grin as the ball pinged into the back of the net.

The room went silent. 'Henry took that chance well, to be fair,' Robert said, trying to sound disappointed.

Liverpool were ahead again before half-time, as Owen scored from a Gerrard pass. 'Owen is so good!'

Niko shouted, hugging his dad.

'Gerrard's pass did all the hard work for him, though,' his dad replied, laughing as Niko cut the hug short and shook his head.

The mood in the room swung again with Arsenal's second equaliser. 2–2.

Robert was still focused on Henry, watching his technique when he had the ball and his movement when he was waiting for a pass. Henry then cushioned a pass with the inside of his foot just beyond the halfway line and began dribbling towards the Arsenal goal. 'Go on! Go on!' Robert felt himself mumbling quietly.

Henry skipped past one defender and sped on to the edge of the box. The Liverpool players backed off, afraid of giving away a penalty, and Robert could hear the buzz of the Arsenal fans sensing something magical was happening. Henry faked a shot, got another defender off balance, and suddenly he was one-on-one with the goalkeeper. As the ball curled into the bottom corner, Niko's dad slumped back on the sofa. 'Someone get a tackle in!' he shouted, throwing his arms in the air.

Robert watched the replay twice and kept quiet. But inside, he could feel himself screaming 'What a goal! What a goal!'

Even before Henry completed his hat-trick a few minutes later, Robert knew this was the player he would look up to for the next few years. Henry had it all – pace, clinical finishing, effortless control – and he could see defenders were terrified of being embarrassed in one-on-one situations. While Robert was not about to share these opinions in front of Niko's dad, he was already thinking about how he could watch other Arsenal games in the weeks ahead.

Robert's connection with Henry was about more than just tuning in for the games, though. Again and again, he found himself copying his new hero in training, with the way he opened up his body to curl the ball into the far corner, just like Henry had done so often. Robert was getting better at timing his runs too and avoiding the offside flag. Like Henry, he was quick enough so that he could be patient with his movement.

As it turned out, 2004 was the year that Arsenal completed their unbeaten Premier League season. Back at Niko's house to watch their final game against Leicester, Robert soaked up every touch and every moment. Henry made being a striker seem even cooler than Baggio and Del Piero had, and Robert wanted to be just like him.

## CHAPTER 8

# THE LEGIA
# SPOTLIGHT

As Robert kept scoring goals in important games,
word spread among youth academies across Poland.
He moved on from Varsovia to Delta Warsaw but
stayed for just one season. With local scouts turning
up regularly to watch Robert's games, Krzysztof had a
feeling that it was only a matter of time before Legia
Warsaw entered the picture.

But all the scouts seemed to have the same question
after seeing Robert in action: was he too skinny to
make it in the physical Polish leagues?

'He's got the pace and the finishing,' one scout
reported back. 'There's no question about that at
all. But he's so thin. He'll get pushed around against

stronger defenders.'

'That boy is a natural goalscorer,' another said. 'I just don't know how far that will take him if he doesn't get stronger.'

Krzysztof always shook his head when he heard these opinions. 'Robert finds other ways to make up for that. Trust me, there are plenty of physical defenders in these youth leagues, and he always gets the better of them.'

These same debates were happening at the mighty Legia Warsaw too. The club had sent three different scouts to watch Robert play and the report cards told a familiar story.

'I get your point about him being too skinny, but that's something that can change with a summer in the gym,' one of the directors said, looking again at the reports on his desk. 'If Robert has all the things you can't teach – good instincts, pace, an eye for goal – then we should bring him to Legia.'

When Krzysztof got the call from Legia, his eyes lit up. He spoke to the club contact for at least ten minutes, then went to find Robert, who was doing homework in his room.

'I've got some incredible news,' Krzysztof said. 'In fact, it's so incredible that you can even take a break from your homework.'

Robert put his pen down and turned around in his chair, giving Krzysztof his full concentration.

'Legia Warsaw just called to invite you to join their academy, son.' When he didn't get the joyful response he was expecting, Krzysztof tried again. He put his hands out with his palms pointing up. 'Come on, this is the biggest club in Poland. Where's the big smile?'

But Robert wasn't so sure. 'I'm just starting to feel settled at Delta,' he told his dad. 'I like the coaches and my teammates have been really welcoming. The idea of giving all that up to join a team where I might not play as much... I... I don't know.'

That left Krzysztof and Iwona in a tricky scenario. They wanted to support Robert on this, but they also knew all about Legia's reputation and resources.

'We just want you to really think about this opportunity,' Iwona explained as the family sat down to discuss the Legia offer again. 'Ever since you were a little boy, you've had big dreams when it comes to football. While some boys just want to become footballers, you've always believed you could become a great player with one of the world's biggest clubs. If that's still your dream, really think about what the Legia spotlight could do for your career.'

As Robert stared at the table, struggling to make up his mind, his dad added: 'This is your decision, Robert. We just want to make sure you have no regrets. If you decide you don't want to do this, I can call Legia in the morning.'

That night, Robert sat up in bed and turned on his lamp. He was never going to fall asleep unless he made up his mind about Legia. As he looked around his room, his eye was drawn to the posters on his wall – an old Baggio one and a newer one of the Poland national team. In that moment, he knew what he wanted to do. Though he didn't feel ready to leave Delta, joining Legia would be another big step towards becoming the kind of superstar that played for his country and ended up on posters in kids' rooms around the world. It was a chance that might never come up again, and he had to take it.

Robert slid out of bed and tiptoed to his parents' room. Their light was still on too. 'Mum, Dad, I know what I need to do,' he said. 'I'm going to give it a shot at Legia.'

'Okay then,' Krzysztof replied. He had been falling asleep reading his book but was now wide awake. 'We'll finish the rest of the arrangements in the morning and Legia are expecting you for your first training session on Thursday.'

As Robert left the room, Krzysztof and Iwona shared a proud smile. Once again, their son had proved that he was willing to do whatever it took to make it to the top.

## CHAPTER 9

# STEPPING UP

The start of a new season was usually a time for excitement in the Lewandowski house, but this year was different. Krzysztof had been ill for months and his doctors had advised the family that there might not be much time left for him.

Eventually, the day they had all been dreading arrived. When Robert and Milena got home from school, Iwona was sitting in the kitchen in tears.

'Did… has… Dad…?' Robert stumbled to find the right words.

Iwona nodded, hugging Robert and Milena and not wanting to let go. She wiped the tears from her cheeks and took a deep breath. 'Let's sit on the sofa,' she said.

Robert didn't know what to say as he sat down with his mum. Tears filled his eyes. 'Was he in pain at the end?' he asked, in a shaky voice.

'No, it was very quick,' she replied. 'It's going to take us some time to figure things out, but the three of us have to keep moving forward. We will never, never, never forget what a wonderful husband and father he was. But he would want us to keep living.'

The three of them sat together on the sofa for what felt like hours. They talked a little, but it was mostly a calm silence – thinking, remembering, processing.

This situation changed everything for Robert. When the illness had become more serious, his dad had told him a few times that he would have to step up to support his mum and Milena as the man of the house. They were all suffering, but life had to go on.

In every sense, Robert had to grow up quickly. He still had the same boyish face of a teenager, but he was taking on the responsibilities of an adult. He was juggling schoolwork, football and extra jobs at home – to the point where Iwona worried that he would fall asleep at his desk.

'My mum and my sister really need my help –
now and in the future,' he told his friends. 'As hard
as things are at the moment, I'm going to be strong
and I'm going to take care of my family.'

Robert knew he could help in a few different
ways – and one of those was through football. If he
continued to shine as a professional footballer, that
would bring financial security for the whole family.
He didn't know exactly how much money the star
players in the top European leagues were paid, but
he was sure it was enough to cover the family's bills.
For now, his Legia wages would at least help.

Robert had always hoped to make it at the
professional level, but now he was determined to
leave nothing to chance. The next week, he started
setting his alarm for 5am every day to fit in a morning
run before school. Then in the evenings, once he had
finished his homework, he would take a ball into the
garden and work on his dribbling.

He often thought about his dad – and the role
that Krzysztof had played in getting him this far. He
had never pushed Robert to become a professional

footballer, nor been one of those parents screaming at their kids from the touchline during games. Instead, as Robert looked back, he recalled his dad's only goal being to see his son doing something he loved. That is what had made their bond so special.

As he dribbled the ball through a couple of cones and pretended to fire a shot into the garden fence, Robert clung to the fact that he could still fulfil the dream – their dream – of becoming a successful footballer. 'I'm going to see it through, Dad,' he whispered to himself as he flicked the ball up and trapped it expertly under his foot.

## CHAPTER 10

# INJURY HEARTBREAK

A few months later, however, Robert's football dream felt a long way away as he lay on the ground, holding his knee and trying to manage the pain. The youth team physio ran over to check on him and did his best to keep Robert calm.

After running through a series of quick checks, the physio helped Robert get back to his feet and over to the touchline. But it was clear that he would not be back on the pitch that afternoon. Robert picked up a training top and put it around his shoulders. The physio appeared again with an ice pack and some tape to keep it in place.

By the end of the game, Robert's knee felt even

worse. He needed to lean on two of his teammates to limp his way back to the dressing room, where he slumped down beside his kitbag. Now what?

Robert was back for a couple of tests early the next week to find out more about the damage to his knee. As usual in these circumstances, he had lots of questions – and the answers would not be available for at least a week.

As he sat down at the side of the training pitch and watched his teammates working on shooting drills, Robert sighed. He was finding out the hard way that injuries could be really lonely experiences.

His phone buzzed in his pocket. It was Milena. 'Hi bro, have you finished the tests yet?' she asked.

'Yep, all done in an hour. That's the easy part, though. Now I've got to wait for the results.'

'Well, luckily for you, I've made a list of things you can do to pass the time,' she said, then giggled. 'I can style your hair for you, you can serve the snacks when my friends come over, and you can do some of my homework.'

Robert laughed. 'So thoughtful of you!'

'Oh, that was just the top three. I've got seven more here.'

They both laughed – and, for a few minutes at least, Robert was distracted from all his worries about his knee.

When the test results arrived, Robert swallowed hard and sat down with the academy doctor. The news was bad – not terrible, but bad. He would not be able to play for two to three months. The doctor left him with a detailed rehab plan and five sheets of exercises that he could try at home once the swelling had settled down.

As Robert digested this news and settled into a routine of lying on the sofa for most of the day, he had another troubling thought. His contract at Legia would soon be expiring and he was still waiting to have more conversations with the club about extending it. What would happen now?

'One step at a time,' Iwona suggested. 'You need to put all your energy into your recovery. Don't overthink the contract. That's a conversation to have with the academy once you're feeling stronger.'

The weeks ticked by and Robert was still uncertain about his future. Why hadn't anyone at Legia called him to discuss his contract? Eventually, he decided to go to the academy for answers.

Iwona dropped him off and waited nervously in the car. She was expecting to wait at least half an hour, and her heart sank when she saw Robert reappear in less than ten minutes. He looked like he'd seen a ghost.

And that was how he felt too. He got back into the car holding a small envelope and burst into tears.

'The coaches didn't even come out to speak to me,' he sobbed. 'The secretary looked up my name and there was this envelope already prepared for me. Legia aren't renewing my contract. That's it.'

Iwona hugged her son, with her heart breaking for Robert and anger rising for the way he had been treated. With everything he had been through, it felt like a cruel way to treat a boy who had always done everything the club asked him to do.

In that moment, Robert felt like his life was falling apart – first, his dad had been taken from him and now, possibly, his football career. He was usually good at finding the positives in any situation but, as he sat up in bed unable to sleep, he couldn't think of any.

'Tomorrow is another day,' he reminded himself as he lay back down on his pillow.

## CHAPTER 11

# STARTING OVER

As much as Robert wanted to stay in bed and take a few days to get over the contract disappointment, Iwona refused to let that happen. Her number one priority was getting Robert back on track.

'Let's move on to what comes next,' she told him, opening the curtains and clapping her hands. 'Forget Legia – they'll regret it one day, but you can't change any of that now.'

'Mum, until my knee has fully recovered, no-one is going to want me.'

'Well not with that attitude, no. We can at least start making some calls. I'm sure there are some exercises you could be doing too, rather than lying in bed.'

Robert groaned and sat up. He knew he wasn't going to win this one.

'Until you're ready to fight, I'll fight for you,' Iwona told him as she walked out of the room. 'You've come too far to walk away now.'

But finding a club was tougher than she had expected. The top teams in Poland had seen him play but still thought he was too skinny to make it at that level, and other teams claimed their squads were already full for next season. Robert's agent, Cezary, was doing his best too.

Finally, they got one team to listen and agree to a contract. But Iwona feared that Robert might not see it as a reason to celebrate.

'Znicz Pruszków?' Robert said, with a shocked look in his eyes. 'They're a Third Division team!'

'Just think about it,' Iwona replied. 'We've spoken with them and they're interested in giving you a chance to prove yourself again.'

'And when you show what a natural goalscorer you are, the offers will come flying in from bigger teams,' Cezary added.

Robert thought about it. The truth was that he was hardly in a position to be picky – he was club-less and recovering from a serious injury. His mood quickly shifted to feeling grateful that Znicz were willing to give him this shot. 'You're right,' he finally said. 'Let's do it. This is just the first stop on my comeback tour.'

But after the first few training sessions, Robert wanted to cry. It was like he was learning football all over again. One minute, he was taking too many touches and wasting a good opportunity to shoot; the next minute, he was rushing a shot and firing it embarrassingly wide. Maybe he had returned from the injury too soon.

In these difficult moments, Robert often thought back to one of his dad's favourite lines when he was having a rough patch – 'trust your instincts'. He worked even harder in training and put in extra hours with anyone who was willing to stand in goal for shooting practice.

As Robert's touch and movement began to feel natural again, the Znicz coaches saw flashes of the player who had seemed to be on the fast track to

Ekstraklasa stardom. 'He looked so sharp today in training,' one of the coaches reported. 'We might have got a real bargain here if he stays fit and plays like that.'

After all the challenges of the past year, Robert was just happy to be back doing what he loved. With every clinical performance in training, he made his case to the Znicz coaches for more playing time – and then he just had to take those opportunities when they arrived.

Robert got the perfect chance away to MG MZKS Kozienice in the eighth game of the season. Znicz took the lead in the first minute and were 4–0 up heading into the last ten minutes, but they kept pushing for more. Tired defenders were no match for Robert as he won the race to a long ball and placed a quick shot into the bottom corner.

*Goooooooooooooooooooaaaaaaaaaaaaaaaaallllllllllllll llllllllllll!!!!!!!!!!!!!!!!!!!*

He jumped and punched the air. It was so good to have the feeling of scoring a goal again.

A minute later, he got another, making a clever near post run and giving the goalkeeper no chance with a glancing header.

*Goooooooooooooooooooooaaaaaaaaaaaaaaaallllllllllllll llllllllllll!!!!!!!!!!!!!!!!!!!!*

He was back! By the end of the season, there was even more reason to celebrate. Znicz clinched promotion to the Second Division and Robert finished as the league's top scorer with fifteen goals.

As the players planned their big end-of-season party, manager Leszek Ojrzyński called Robert to his office. 'I just want you to know how impressed I was with you this season. You came here during a difficult time and your attitude was spot-on from day one. Even the older players quickly saw that you were willing to put in the work to help the team.'

'Thanks, boss. That means a lot. Znicz gave me just what I needed at a time when I felt things spinning out of control.'

'Well, it worked out well for everyone,' Leszek added, smiling. 'And we'll need even more from you next season if we're going to stay afloat in the Second Division. So get some rest and I'll see you in July.'

Robert felt he had the momentum back in his career

again. After a few weeks off, he was back in the gym and running laps at the training ground to get into the best possible shape ahead of the new season. 'Defences in the Second Division are sure to be quicker and stronger,' he explained to Milena when he turned up late for lunch after a morning workout. 'I'll need to be at my best.'

As Leszek had hinted, Robert would have an even bigger role in his second year at Znicz, and he made the perfect start with goals in the first two league games as he and Bartosz Wiśniewski, another youngster trying to prove himself, left defenders in the dust.

'If we keep playing like this, there's no reason why we can't get promoted again,' Bartosz said as they warmed up together for their next game away to GKS Katowice.

Robert smiled. 'One game at a time, my friend. But I think we're already proving a lot of people wrong. Some of the previews said we'd be in a relegation battle all year.'

GKS Katowice quickly became the latest team to

be picked apart by Robert and Bartosz. It only took Robert sixteen minutes to score one of his trademark goals – a ball bounced in the penalty area, the defenders hesitated, and he was onto it in a flash, sliding to poke a quick shot past the goalkeeper.

*Goooooooooooooooooooaaaaaaaaaaaaaaaaalllllllllllllll lllllllllllll!!!!!!!!!!!!!!!!!!!*

Robert picked himself off the floor and glided away to celebrate as his teammates joined him by the corner flag.

'It's like you know what's going to happen ahead of time,' Bartosz said as they walked back to the halfway line. 'You're always the first to get to those 50-50 balls.'

'You snooze, you lose,' Robert replied, laughing.

Even as Znicz went through some tougher patches, Robert was still finding the net regularly and drawing more attention from Ekstraklasa clubs. He had a knack for scoring key goals too, including an equaliser against Arka Gdynia with the last kick of the game.

Though the Znicz promotion charge fell just short, Robert added another league top scorer award to his trophy collection, finishing on twenty-one goals.

Within days of the end of the season, Znicz began to receive calls from clubs – both from the Ekstraklasa, Poland's top league, and abroad – desperate to sign Robert. It was clear that he belonged at a higher level and Znicz were willing to make a deal for the right price. Eventually, Lech Poznań won the race for Robert, setting up the next chapter in his career.

As he said goodbye to his Znicz teammates, he reflected on what his two seasons at the club had meant to him. Basically, they had saved him at a time when he wasn't even sure about continuing with football. Now, he had found his way, and this new adventure would pit him against the best defenders in the country. He felt ready.

## CHAPTER 12

# ANNA

Robert's time at Znicz Pruszków hadn't just turned
his fortunes around on the pitch, it had changed
his life forever off the pitch too. At the end of his
first season, he registered to attend a session at the
University of Warsaw's School of Education in Sports.
Iwona had insisted that Robert keep an open mind
about studying to ensure he had a backup plan if his
football career faltered.

At first, Robert questioned the need to disrupt his
summer with schoolwork, but he found himself more
interested than he'd expected as he walked into the
hall. It felt good to be focusing on something other
than football for once.

As he waited for the session to start, Robert wandered over to the refreshments stand.

'Can I get you a coffee?' asked a tall man with short blond hair. Robert could hear the same question being asked in the queues next to him.

'No, thank you – just a bottle of water please,' Robert replied.

From the line to his right, he heard a young woman give the exact same answer.

'Any snacks today, sir?'

'I'll have one of the granola bars, please.' Again, the same answer came from the next queue.

He looked over, just as the young woman was looking over at him. She was very pretty and seemed to be about the same age as him. They locked eyes and laughed.

'You've got good taste,' she said, holding up her water and granola bar.

Robert immediately felt his cheeks going red. He fumbled for his wallet and, as he reached to pay, he knocked his water bottle on the floor. He scuttled away to pick up a programme and cool down.

When the main doors to the hall opened, Robert was texting his mum to let her know he was at the session and would come over to her house afterwards. He let the crowd of people trickle into the room and then quickly finished his granola bar so that he wouldn't be crunching during the entire session.

By the time he walked into the hall, the main presenter was at the podium beginning his presentation. 'Quick, sit down,' a voice whispered from a row on the left. It was the young woman from the refreshments stand, and she was pointing to a chair next to her. Well, I can't make a bigger fool of myself than I already have, Robert thought, as he walked over. He left a seat in between them to give her some space.

'I've heard this guy is a real character,' she said quietly. 'He usually picks on people who arrive late when he needs volunteers.'

'Then thanks for saving me,' he whispered back. A special appearance on the stage was the last thing he needed. 'I'm Robert, by the way.'

'I'm Anna,' she replied. 'Nice to meet you.'

Robert spent the first hour of the session half-listening to the presentation and half-thinking about things he could say to impress Anna. He kicked himself for not making more of an effort to look good that morning – at least he'd had a shower.

At the first break, Anna slid over to the seat next to Robert. 'So, no coffee, no doughnuts,' she said. 'What's that all about?'

Robert smiled. 'I could ask you the same question.'

'I asked you first,' Anna replied, grinning.

'I'm a professional footballer,' he answered. 'I'm playing for Znicz Pruskówat the moment, but hopefully this is just the start.'

Anna gave him a long look. Robert couldn't tell if she was deciding whether to believe him or if she just didn't like his answer.

'What about you?'

'The same kind of reason,' she replied. 'I'm training to represent Poland in karate, so taking care of my body is a big deal.'

'Wow, that's… that's great,' Robert said, trying not to sound too surprised. 'I'll be on my best behaviour now that I know that!'

Anna smiled. 'I'm applying here to study nutrition,' she added. 'It's something I've always been interested in and I can't do karate forever.'

'Well, they'd be mad not to offer you a place,' Robert said. 'And very brave!'

The next speaker was now at the podium and the room fell silent again.

At the end of the session, Anna picked up her bag and put away her notepad and pen. Robert took a sip of water for extra courage and then stood up.

'Would you like to go out for dinner some time, Anna?' he asked nervously. 'With me, I mean, in case that wasn't clear.'

'Thanks for confirming that!' she said, laughing. Then she turned serious. 'How do I know you're not like some of the other footballers I've heard about who haven't turned out to be the nicest guys?'

'Well, let me prove I'm different,' he replied. 'I'll even make sure the food is suitable for a future nutritionist!'

Anna smiled. 'Well, how can I say no to that?! Pass

me your phone and I'll give you my number.'

Robert tried to play it cool, but he couldn't stop grinning. 'Are you free on Saturday?' he asked.

'Yes, I am. Any time after two. Where are we going?'

'It's a surprise,' Robert said quickly. He had no idea and wanted a few days to come up with a plan.

Robert knew he needed some help to plan the perfect date, so he asked his mum and Milena for ideas during their family supper that night.

'Ooooooh,' Milena immediately said, giggling at how uncomfortable her brother looked. 'You're all embarrassed.'

'No, I'm not!' Robert shot back. 'I just don't want to mess it up. Anna is really nice.'

In the end, he decided on a picnic in one of his favourite parks. With help with Iwona and Milena, Robert had thought of everything – a blanket, bottles of water, fresh bread, cheeses, strawberries, salad and meats.

'I have to say, I'm impressed,' Anna said when she saw what Robert had prepared. 'This is perfect.' She picked up a bottle of water and sat down next to him.

As they made sandwiches and watched the sunset, Robert didn't want the evening to end. They talked about all kinds of things – even things that he usually kept bottled up inside – and made plans for a second date the next weekend.

The more time they spent together, the more Robert could picture their life together, chasing their sports dreams. Everything was better with Anna around – and he could tell she felt the same way about him. As Robert thought about the path ahead in his football career, he loved that he now had a partner for that journey.

# CHAPTER 13

# POLISH
# PRIDE

From the very first training session with Lech, Robert
was aware that he might have to wait his turn for
playing time, with a strong group of strikers battling
for minutes. But manager Franciszek Smuda saw
enough to throw him straight into the squad when
the 2008–09 season kicked off.

'You've shown in preseason that you can handle
the physical side of the game,' Franciszek explained.
'That was my only worry. With the way we play,
you're going to get lots of chances – so just make
sure you bring the same shooting boots you were
wearing today.'

Robert smiled. He had smashed in three screamers

in training, including the winner in their eight v eight game.

Robert started on the bench but, as he ran onto the pitch as a second-half substitute, he felt the hairs on the back of his neck standing on end. Everything was more impressive in the Ekstraklasa – the crowds were louder, the dressing rooms were cleaner, the pitches were greener. He just hoped that the defenders weren't that much better.

The night before, while chatting with an old Varsovia teammate, Robert had pointed out that making a good start would really help him settle at Lech. And sure enough, he scored on his league debut! As Lech attacked down the right wing, Robert waited patiently before making his move. The cross was driven low and he was a step ahead of his marker with a sharp near post run and an even better flicked finish.

*Goooooooooooooooooooooaaaaaaaaaaaaaaaaaalllllllllllllll lllllllllll!!!!!!!!!!!!!!!!!!!!*

'Now that's a proper debut goal!' shouted his strike partner, Hernán Rengifo.

With five goals in his first five games, Robert

made the perfect start. The pressure was off, and he was finding that he could still get the extra yard of space he needed, even against Ekstraklasa defences. Growing stronger every week, Robert's goals – eighteen in total – kept Lech in the title race. Though they finished third, five points behind the champions, Wisła Kraków, he was sure Lech could find an extra gear to go all the way next season.

Robert's form for Lech was the talk of the Ekstraklasa, and more and more people were taking note. He knew he was playing well but still saw plenty of ways that he could get better. After all, he had only just turned twenty.

One morning, Robert was visiting his mum and washing the plates after lunch. He heard his phone ringing in the living room. 'Mum, please can you answer that? Just take a message or tell them I'll call them back in five minutes.'

Iwona took the call and needed every last bit of self-control not to let out an excited scream. She ran into the kitchen.

Robert looked confused. 'I thought you were

going to…'

Iwona was shaking her head. 'Son, you're going to want to take this call right now. It's Leo Beenhakker.'

The Poland national team manager. Robert dried his hands in a hurry and took the phone.

'Hi, sorry about that,' he said quickly.

'No problem,' Leo said, laughing. 'Is your mum okay? I think I gave her a bit of a shock!'

Robert laughed too. 'Yes, she's recovering now! Don't worry, this will give her a story to tell her friends for weeks.'

'Okay, good! You can probably guess why I'm calling. Later today, I'll be announcing the national team squad to play San Marino, and I just wanted to reach out personally to let you know that you'll be in it. Congratulations.'

Robert had to lean on the kitchen counter as his legs turned to jelly. He had played for the Poland Under-21 team but assumed it would be a much longer wait before he made his debut for the senior team. 'Wow, erm… thank you! I… I've always dreamed of playing for my country. This is such an honour.'

'You've earned it. We've been watching you closely over the past eighteen months – and I've got a feeling that you're going to be putting on the Poland shirt for many years to come.'

Iwona listened from the doorway. When Robert ended the call, she wrapped him in a big hug. 'I'm so proud of you,' she said. 'And I'm sure your dad is smiling right now too.'

To say that Robert was nervous as he arrived at the hotel to join the rest of the Poland squad would be an understatement. After dropping off his suitcase, he followed the directions to the meeting room. When he walked into the room, he froze. In the back row of seats, he saw two of his idols, Jacek Bąk and Maciej Żurawski.

They turned to face Robert just as he was picking up his copy of the team notes from the main table.

'Sorry, this is going to sound silly, but I looked up to you both so much growing up,' Robert said when they saw him staring. 'I can't believe I'm standing here next to you as part of the Poland squad.'

'Well, now I feel really old. How about you, Jacek?'

Maciej said.

Robert felt his face go bright red. 'Oh sorry, I didn't mean to...'

'Don't worry, I'm only joking! Welcome to the squad!'

The room went quiet when the coaches walked in, and Robert hung on every word as Leo walked through the game plan.

'Even if I don't play a minute tomorrow, this has been an unbelievable experience,' Robert told Milena as he tried to calm his nerves.

He felt incredible pride as he stood for the national anthems then carried his Number 13 shirt to sit down with the other substitutes. He had to pinch himself to believe that he was really here representing his country.

Early in the second half, with Poland 1–0 up, Leo looked at Robert and waved him over. 'Keep warming up and we'll get you on up front in five minutes.'

Robert gave the most confident nod he could manage with all the nerves floating around. He stretched his calves and his hamstrings, jumped up and down a couple of times and took a long sip of water. Showtime!

One of the assistant coaches gave the signal and Robert jogged over, taking off his warm-up top. 'Play on the shoulder of the last defender and look for the through ball,' the coach explained. 'San Marino are playing a high line so there's room in behind.'

The electronic board went up, showing that Number 13 was coming on. As Robert ran onto the pitch, Maciej came over and put his arm round his shoulders. 'Just play your game. These guys will be terrified of your pace and movement, so take them on whenever you can.'

It only took eight minutes for Robert to make his mark. A low shot bounced back off the post and he was the first to react, darting in to poke the ball into the net.

*Goooooooooooooooooooooaaaaaaaaaaaaaaaaalllllllllllllll lllllllllllll!!!!!!!!!!!!!!!!!!*

Robert spun away to celebrate, and Maciej jumped on his back. 'Talk about an instant impact!' he said. 'That's a goal you'll never forget.'

At the final whistle, just when Robert thought this night could not get any more unbelievable, one of the

Poland staff called him over. 'They want you for a TV interview,' she said. 'Follow me.'

Before he knew it, Robert was in front of a camera, recapping his goal and explaining what it meant to make his Poland debut. 'This is a dream that I'm not ready to wake up from,' he said, grinning.

Back in the dressing room, Robert's new teammates had a little surprise waiting for him. When he walked in, they all had cups of water ready, drenching him and then wrapping him in hugs.

Leo appeared with a towel. 'Sorry, they insisted on a proper celebration,' he said, laughing. 'That was a great debut and the first of many international goals, I'm sure.'

## CHAPTER 14

# WINNING TIME

Back at Lech, a slow start to the season meant
Robert and his teammates were facing questions over
whether they could really match Wisła and Legia.
An October clash with Wisla was a chance to make
a statement and, as Robert sat in the dressing room
putting on his shinpads, that was exactly the thought
going through his head.

'We've got to show we're in this title race for
the long haul,' he said to Hector, who was already
bubbling with pre-game excitement. 'If we win today,
we're right in the mix.'

Hector nodded. 'Yes, sir! It's going to be a battle.
We'll even need you to get stuck in today!'

Robert laughed. 'You know I like to keep my kit clean.'

As Hector had predicted, it was a tight game with very few chances. Robert made three good runs behind the defence and each time the pass was just too long. Still, he gave his teammates a thumbs up. There was space for through balls and, at some point, they would get the timing just right.

Early in the second half, the ball dropped to Hector. As soon as his teammate had it under control, Robert sprinted into a gap. Hector poked a pass for him to run onto and Robert was through on goal for the first time all game. He took one touch, glanced at where the goalkeeper was, and then fired the ball beyond his reach. The fans were already screaming before the ball nestled in the back of the net.

*Goooooooooooooooooooooaaaaaaaaaaaaaaaalllllllllllll llllllllllll!!!!!!!!!!!!!!!!!!*

Robert ran over to the Lech fans with his arms out like wings. 'Well, you could hardly miss with a perfect pass like that!' Hector shouted in his ear, laughing.

Back in the dressing room, new Lech boss Jacek

Zieliński went round shaking hands with every player. 'Fantastic performance, lads,' he said. 'Celebrate this one. You really should – it takes a lot to beat a team like Wisła. But let's make this the springboard for the rest of the season. If we don't show up next week, this was all for nothing.'

Robert felt the mood of the squad had shifted that afternoon. Lech had proved they could beat anyone on their day, and that new-found confidence made them unstoppable, kickstarting a long unbeaten run in the league.

Heading into the last two weeks of the season, Lech were trailing Wisła by just one point at the top of the Ekstraklasa. There was no margin for error and, as tired as Robert was, there could be no excuses. They needed two more wins and a bit of help from Wisła's opponents.

When Lech fell behind just after half-time away to Ruch Chorzów, their title dreams were hanging by a thread. But Robert willed his teammates back into the game. He made more runs, he dropped deeper to get on the ball, and he found himself shouting encouragement more than he had ever done before. Then he scored the equaliser. Lech moved the ball well down the right and Robert was in the right place at the right time to tap the cross home.

*Goooooooooooooooooooooaaaaaaaaaaaaaaaaallllllllllllll llllllllllllll!!!!!!!!!!!!!!!!!!!!*

He ran to grab the ball out of the net to save a few extra seconds. Lech kept pushing forward in search of a winner, taking risks defensively to try to create one last chance. As Robert battled to get on the end of a cross, Siergiej Kriwiec popped up as the hero, scoring in the ninetieth minute to spark wild celebrations.

'We're still in it!' Robert yelled as they all jumped on Siergiej. 'We're not done yet.'

Back in the dressing room, news filtered through that there was late drama in Wisła's game too, with the leaders conceding a late equaliser. Lech had leapfrogged them into first place, taking a one-point lead!

That set up a dramatic final day of the season, and Robert had trouble sleeping all week with a childhood dream within touching distance. If Lech won at home to Zagłębie Lubin, they would be crowned champions.

Jacek looked around the dressing room as the clock on the wall showed that there were just twenty minutes until kick-off. 'This is a day for calm heads,' he said. 'You've all worked incredibly hard to get into this position. Don't overcomplicate it now. Keep the shape defensively, ping the ball around, and look for the direct pass up to Robert when it's available. One more big performance – that's all we need.'

Robert felt like he could run through a wall. Whatever happened, he would leave every ounce of energy out there on the pitch. At half-time, Lech had a 1–0 lead, but word soon leaked through that Wisła were also 1–0 up. Robert took a deep breath as he walked down the tunnel for the second half. 'Time to finish the job,' he mumbled to himself.

He waited patiently as another Lech attack developed through the midfield and then out to the left wing. Robert saw Hector making the near post run and held his position around the penalty spot. The cross was meant for Hector but bounced up off a defender – and there was only ever one outcome with loose balls in the box. Robert spotted his chance immediately and pounced to hammer the ball into the roof of the net.

*Goooooooooooooooooooaaaaaaaaaaaaaaaaaallllllllllllll llllllllllll!!!!!!!!!!!!!!!!!!!*

He skidded on his knees and was soon buried in blue Lech shirts. They were so close now.

Jacek couldn't stand still on the touchline. After celebrating Robert's goal, he was soon barking instructions to the rest of the team and demanding a more cautious approach. Lech survived a few goalmouth scrambles and, at last, the final whistle sounded. Robert jumped and punched the air. He ran over to join his teammates.

'*Campeones, Campeones, Olé! Olé! Olé!*' they sang as the fans danced and hugged. To make the celebrations even sweeter, one of the assistant coaches reminded Robert that his eighteen Ekstraklasa goals made him the league's top scorer.

The party went on late into the night, and Robert savoured every moment. Most of all, he remembered the feeling of holding the trophy in his hands and raising it to the fans. It was something he would never forget but, as the summer rolled along, he was soon thinking about chasing the next trophy.

## CHAPTER 15

# THE KLOPP FACTOR

In 2010, Robert's form for Lech did not stay a secret for long, as European clubs jockeyed for position to sign him. But one team stood out for Robert from the beginning – Borussia Dortmund in Germany. Cezary kept him updated on the latest developments and it was flattering to see so much interest. The universe seemed to be nudging Robert towards Dortmund, with a possible move to Blackburn in the UK called off because the volcanic ash from the eruption of Eyjafjallajökull in Iceland made air travel impossible for a time in northern and western Europe.

When Cezary confirmed that Dortmund had made an official offer, Robert punched the air in joy and relief.

This felt like the big break he had been working towards.

Robert called his mum to tell her that the transfer would soon be made public. As he hung up, his phone buzzed again with a number he didn't recognise. 'Hello?' he said.

'Hi Robert, it's Jürgen Klopp at Dortmund,' answered the voice. 'I'm sure you've got a lot of calls to make and plans to figure out, but let me be the first to say how thrilled we are to be adding you to our squad. We've got big plans for the next few years and I'm confident that you'll be a big part of those.'

Robert couldn't stop grinning. 'Thanks, boss. That's great to hear. I can't wait to get started.'

'We're going to push you hard, but only because we believe in your potential. The number one thing I want you to know is that we're a family at Dortmund. I really care about my players and we're going to have some fun along the way.' Jürgen chuckled – a chuckle that Robert would hear again and again over the next few years.

Swapping Poland for Germany meant Robert would be more alone than ever before. For all the excitement about the opportunities he would have on the pitch, part of him worried about the adjustment. 'It's a lot of change all at once,' he explained to Milena. 'A new place to live, a different language, no family, no friends. I guess I'm just a bit nervous about taking this step, even though I know I want to do it. Does that make any sense?'

'It does, and it's natural,' his sister replied. 'We'll be there to visit you as often as we can, and you'll learn things quickly… washing, cooking, the language barrier. Just don't be afraid to ask Dortmund for help to get settled.'

'Yes, I'll be speaking with a few different people from the club over the next week and I've got a list of things to ask.'

But when Anna managed to change her plans so that she could join him, Robert felt ten times better.

Even so, adjusting to life in Germany was even tougher than he had expected. The intensity of Klopp's training sessions caught him by surprise, with his manager roaming the pitch and barking instructions. 'Press, press, press!' 'Again, again, move the ball.'

'Come on, Robert. Dig deep and win it back.'

The other players were so skilful too. Even the defenders had quick feet and looked comfortable in the one-touch drills. Robert was one of several youngsters in the squad, which made life a little easier. He quickly became friends with Mario Götze, who was also settling into the first team.

Jürgen demanded a lot from his players, but Robert also got to see the softer side. 'How are you settling in Dortmund?' Jürgen would often ask. 'Is there anything you need?'

A few months into Robert's first season, Jürgen pulled him aside at the end of training. 'Take your time on the ball. I know your instinct is to do everything fast and slick, but don't be afraid to slow things down. An extra touch can open up other passes.'

That helped. As Robert slowed down his decisions a little, his confidence grew. He still had the aches and pains almost every morning, but increasingly he felt like he belonged. Without even realising it at first, he started hitting first time passes and shots again. This time, he was clinical.

As much as Robert wanted to impress his manager and become a consistent goalscorer in the Bundesliga, he trusted Jürgen's patient approach. Robert, or 'Lewy' as everyone now called him, was mostly used as a substitute in his first season and usually not in his favourite position of central striker. 'Give the Number 10 role a chance,' Jürgen explained. 'I know you're used to being in the box and making runs behind the defence, but you've got the touch and vision to play deeper too.'

'No problem,' Robert replied. He was more than willing to do whatever it took to help the team.

After being very shy in his first few training sessions, Robert soon came out of his shell. He was no longer star-struck by sharing a pitch with Mats Hummels, and it helped to have fellow Pole Jakub Błaszczykowski in the squad.

As Dortmund prepared for their derby showdown with Schalke 04, Jürgen told Robert to stay ready. 'I'm not going to start you in the derby, but you'll be the ace up my sleeve in the second half. You're the last person anyone would want to mark with tired legs late in the game.'

True to his word, Jürgen sent Robert on for the final fifteen minutes, with Dortmund 2–0 up. 'The game is stretched, Lewy,' Jürgen explained. 'Look for the outlet ball and lead the counter-attack.'

Robert raced around, closing down defenders and surging forward to protect the lead. With four minutes to go, Dortmund won a corner. Robert jogged into the box and moved around to confuse his marker. He picked up the flight of the ball instantly and knew he had a chance of reaching it. He planted his feet and timed his jump perfectly, heading the ball down and into the far corner.

*Goooooooooooooooooooooaaaaaaaaaaaaaaaaaallllllllllllll llllllllllll!!!!!!!!!!!!!!!!!!!*

Jürgen was up hugging his assistant coaches. His substitute had delivered the knockout blow. Robert's head was spinning – after the game, he could hardly remember his goal celebration. It was all a blur. He had scored his first league goal – and in the derby, no less.

Dortmund clinched the Bundesliga title in Robert's

first season, and he was learning at a rapid pace. His German was improving and so was his understanding of how Jürgen wanted his team to play.

Robert spoke to Jürgen again at the end of the season to get his manager's thoughts on what he could do during the summer break ahead of next season. 'I'm going to keep working on my strength. I know that's important. But what other areas do you think I should focus on?'

'A little more strength, sure,' Jürgen replied. 'Maybe some heading. But it's just as important to work on what's up here.' He tapped the side of his head. 'You have to believe that you can become one of the best strikers in the world. I believe it and I'm going to keep pushing you to help you get there.'

Robert beamed. It was the perfect ending to his first season at Dortmund, and he sensed that even better years lay ahead.

## CHAPTER 16

# HITTING HIS
# STRIDE

The start of Robert's second season in Dortmund
could not have felt more different than his first. He
had overcome a lot of obstacles in the past twelve
months, from the language barrier to a new country
to new teammates. Now he was ready to take off
and become someone that Jürgen could rely on. But
there would be plenty of competition for playing time,
especially with İlkay Gündoğan and Ivan Perišić
joining Dortmund that summer.

As he stood on the edge of the 'rondo' next to Mario
and also Shinji Kagawa, keeping the ball away from
Mats in the middle, Robert felt stronger and sharper –
and it didn't take long for his teammates to notice.

'Someone's been hitting the gym!' Mario said. 'What's your secret?'

'It's all thanks to Anna,' Robert replied. With Anna's expert advice, he had worked hard on his body during the offseason. He was more careful about what he ate and had committed to a workout routine that added muscle without slowing him down.

When Lucas Barrios, Dortmund's first-choice striker, came back from international duty with Paraguay nursing a thigh injury, Jürgen knew that this was Robert's moment. 'When I said you'd get more chances this season, I wasn't expecting it to happen quite like this,' Jürgen said. 'But we're going to be counting on you in the central striker role.'

'Looking back, I wasn't ready last season,' Robert admitted. 'But I definitely am now.'

He was bursting with excitement as he left the training ground, picturing what it would be like to become a true Dortmund legend.

'I've basically got a trial run in the team for the next few months,' he explained to his mum as he drove home. 'This is my chance to show how far I've come since last season.'

But Dortmund got off to a slow start, with three losses in their first six league games. Though Robert had scored two goals, there was an adjustment period as new teammates got to know the runs he liked to make.

'We just need to get a few wins under our belt to start turning things around,' he told Milena when she called to check on how her brother was handling the pressure. 'You can see it in training and in flashes during games. Once we put it all together, we're going to get on a winning run.'

Bayern Munich were always the likeliest title contender for Dortmund to worry about, but they weren't the only ones: Schalke, Bayer Leverkusen and Borussia Mönchengladbach all had strong squads and star power.

As Robert walked onto the pitch to warm up with Shinji and Mario before the home game against FC Augsburg, he dribbled the ball – left foot, left foot, right foot, right foot. He looked over at the goal and visualised scoring a game-winning header. Dortmund were normally such an attacking, high-scoring team but things hadn't clicked yet this season, and Robert was determined to change that.

He responded with a clinical hat-trick – first, a simple first-time shot, then a swivelling strike with two defenders closing him down and finally a well-placed header. Dortmund suddenly looked like themselves again, with relentless waves of attacking football. The unbeaten run gathered momentum, and Robert couldn't stop scoring, He added two more against 1. FC Köln and one apiece against Wolfsburg, Schalke and Borussia Mönchengladbach.

Even with Lucas fit again, Jürgen continued to trust Robert as his lone striker.

By the time Dortmund were preparing to welcome Bayern in April 2012, their quest to win back-to-back titles was heating up. 'Don't ease off now!' Jürgen pleaded as his players went through their final stretches. 'If you bring the usual intensity from the start, we can take another big step towards our goal today.'

'You can also be sure Bayern haven't forgotten that we beat them at their place earlier in the season,'

Mats added.

Robert heard every word but stayed quiet. He preferred to get into his own zone, especially before big games. Bayern had so much star power, and Robert was reminded of that as he stood across from Arjen Robben and Bastian Schweinsteiger in the tunnel. 'If we get the three points today, we'll deserve to be champions,' he mumbled to himself.

A tight game was still locked at 0–0 late in the second half when Dortmund won a corner. They played it short and the cross was headed clear. Robert jogged back to stay onside. As the ball went back towards the goal, Robert decided in a flash that the shot would have enough power to beat the goalkeeper. In a moment of magic, he flicked the ball as it went through his legs, changing the direction and steering it into the bottom corner.

*Goooooooooooooooooooaaaaaaaaaaaaaaaallllllllllllll lllllllllll!!!!!!!!!!!!!!!!!!!*

The Dortmund fans were on their feet. A second straight title was in sight.

A month later, the two teams were in action again

in the German Cup final. By then, Dortmund had clinched the Bundesliga title, and Robert felt an even bigger part of it this time. Now he was eager to get the party started again with another trophy. With a 2–1 lead just before half-time, Robert saw Shinji Kagawa latch onto a loose ball. 'Play me in, Shinji,' he shouted, as he sprinted ahead of his marker. The pass was perfect and Robert drove a first-time shot into the net.

*Goooooooooooooooooooooaaaaaaaaaaaaaaaaaallllllllllllll llllllllllll!!!!!!!!!!!!!!!!!!!!*

As Bayern kept pushing forward in the second half, Robert knew the next goal would be crucial – if Bayern got it, it would set up a nervy finish; if Dortmund got it, they could clinch the trophy. Again, Shinji got free in midfield and launched the counter-attack, finding Mario bursting forward on the left. Mario spotted Robert peeling away from his marker and slipped a clever pass through Schweinsteiger's legs. Just like in shooting practice, Robert took a touch to open up his body and fired home an unstoppable strike.

*Gooooooooooooooooooooaaaaaaaaaaaaaaaalllllllllllllll
llllllllllllllll!!!!!!!!!!!!!!!!!!!!!!*

Robert jogged away, running backwards as his
teammates chased after him. Surely that was it!

But Bayern pulled a goal back, forcing Robert to
drop back and help the midfield more. With ten
minutes to go, he struck the final blow. A Bayern
mistake led to a floated cross to the back post, and
Robert rose to head in the simplest chance for his
hat-trick.

*Gooooooooooooooooooooaaaaaaaaaaaaaaaalllllllllllllll
llllllllllllllll!!!!!!!!!!!!!!!!!!!!!!*

Jürgen and the substitutes were standing on the
touchline now, arms around each other. As the game
ended, they all raced onto the pitch and formed a big
yellow-and-black circle, singing and jumping.

*'Campeones, Campeones, Olé! Olé! Olé!'*

A league and cup double. What a season! As Robert
prepared to join up with the Poland squad for Euro
2012, he felt like he was on the form of his life.

## CHAPTER 17

# EURO AGONY

'It's always special to be back in Poland,' Robert told Anna when he called from the team's Euro 2012 hotel base. 'There were fans waiting to welcome us when our plane arrived, and more lined up outside the hotel.'

'Well, this is probably a once-in-a-lifetime moment for most of them,' Anna replied. 'Co-hosting Euro 2012 is a big deal. Just wait until you hear how noisy the fans are when you get on the pitch! I can't wait to cheer you on.'

After a good week of preparation, Robert and the rest of the Poland squad felt ready for the tests ahead. Boss Franciszek Smuda, who Robert knew well from his Lech days, had drilled them on the game plan and everyone understood their roles.

'Wow, I see you've brought your Dortmund form with you!' goalkeeper Wojciech Szczęsny shouted, picking the ball out of the net after Robert thumped a volley in off the post during shooting practice. 'Save some of those for the tournament, though!' Thankfully, as the co-hosts, Poland did not have long to wait for their first game. They would be kicking off the tournament against Greece.

On gameday, every moment felt more special. Robert's red Number 9 shirt looked even more impressive, the pitch was impossibly green and inviting, and the feel of the ball was better than ever as he took some practice shots.

With just fifteen minutes before kick-off, Franciszek called for silence in the dressing room, and the players turned to listen to their manager. 'Playing for your country is an experience that very few players get, and you're about to do it at the European Championships in front of your own fans,' he said. 'Savour the moment and play with a smile on your face. Let's start on the front foot and use the crowd for an extra push.'

By the time the national anthems finished and the referee blew the whistle, Robert was desperate to get started. This was it! The whole country would be glued to their TVs for the next two hours, hoping that Poland could feed off their energy.

They made the perfect start, forcing a misplaced pass and counterattacking at pace. Robert watched Jakub Błaszczykowski race down the right wing and tried to guess where the ball might land. He got between two defenders and, as the ball sailed through the air towards him, Robert instantly knew that this was a goalscoring chance. With no defenders near enough to stop his run, he jumped to power a header into the bottom corner.

*Goooooooooooooooooooooaaaaaaaaaaaaaaaaalllllllllllllll llllllllllll!!!!!!!!!!!!!!!!!!*

What a moment! The emotions hit him all at once. Luckily, his teammates were soon racing over to celebrate. Robert looked up into the crowd as he jogged back to the centre circle. It was a sea of red, with chants of Polska! Polska! Polska! He knew Anna was up there somewhere.

When a red card left Greece facing more than forty-five minutes with ten men, the Poland fans sang even louder.

The second half was a different story, though – and Robert felt for Wojciech, who had two nightmare moments. First, he came flying out for a cross and missed it, setting up the Greece equaliser. Less than twenty minutes later, Robert had his hands over his eyes as Wojciech came off his line again and this time gave away a penalty. The referee brought out the red card and suddenly a likely win was heading towards a loss.

Substitute keeper Pzremysław Tytoń jogged onto the pitch and Robert ran over to give him a fist bump. 'You've got this!' he told him. 'This is your moment.'

Robert would later look back on this game as one of the wildest of his whole career. To add to the drama, Pzremysław dived to his left and saved the penalty as Poland clung on for a point.

'Well, where do I start after a game like that?' Franciszek said. The whole dressing room burst out laughing. 'Seriously, though, this was always going to be a tricky game, with the crowd so hyped up and the nerves of kicking off the tournament at home. You rolled with the punches and should be proud of that performance.'

As hard as Franciszek and Robert tried to keep the mood light in training, there was no escaping the pressure heading into their second group game against Russia. 'The whole country is cheering you on,' Anna reminded him one night when he called from his hotel room. 'Turn that into a positive thing. Don't let it become something that weighs you down.'

Once again, the Poland fans made sure it felt like a home game at the National Stadium in Warsaw, and Robert felt a shiver of excitement as they walked down the tunnel. He was in the thick of the action from the start, almost getting on the end of a dangerous free kick and then smashing a left-footed volley just over the bar. 'Almost a goal of the tournament contender!' Jakub called out from behind him.

Robert's quick feet and vision then created a chance for Eugen Polanski, who drilled a low shot into the net. But the offside flag cut the celebrations short.

'Let's get one here!' Robert shouted, sensing that Poland were on top. 'A goal is coming.'

Unfortunately, it came at the other end as Russia took the lead from a free kick. Robert felt sick. Poland had been the better team and now they were behind. But there was a long way to go. At half-time, he went over to each of his teammates and delivered a simple message: 'Win your individual battle and we'll get back in this game.'

Robert played his part. As Jakub pounced on a loose ball, Robert made a run to draw defenders away. Jakub powered into that space and thumped an unstoppable equaliser into the top corner. 'You beauty!' Robert yelled as the whole team ran over to the corner flag.

For the second straight game, Poland had to settle for a point, but this gutsy comeback had everyone in the dressing room believing again. 'Qualification is still in our hands,' Robert told his teammates. 'If we win our last game, we'll be in the quarter-finals for the first time.'

So it all came down to a showdown with the Czech Republic. 'Stay composed and play our way,'

Franciszek said as the players laced their boots and finished taping their ankles.

Just like against Greece and Russia, Poland started well. Robert flashed a good early chance wide on his left foot and shook his head, hoping that he hadn't wasted his best chance of the game. The stadium got quieter and tenser in the second half, then all but silent as the Czechs took the lead with less than twenty minutes to go.

As Poland's desperate late rally fell short, Robert knew his Euro 2012 dream was over. The Czech players sprinted off to celebrate, leaving Robert to pick some of his teammates up off the ground and trudge back to the dressing room. The players were crushed, the fans were crushed – this was not how Robert had pictured their tournament ending.

'You gave it everything,' Franciszek insisted. 'It just wasn't meant to be for us this year.'

But it still stung badly. Robert knew they had created enough chances over the three games and should have had more than two points.

It was a pain that would linger all summer. 'I just

can't shake the feeling that we let the country down,' he told Anna as he fidgeted on the sofa. 'The fans deserved better.'

'You didn't let anyone down,' she said, sitting down next to him. 'Look at me – no-one is saying that. You made a lot of people proud with the way you played. Think about it. You could have won all three of those games, but the luck didn't go your way.'

Robert shrugged, then nodded.

'All you can do now is focus on the positives,' Anna added. 'There are kids all over the country with an even bigger love for football now. You helped to make that happen. Now you've got to keep moving forward.'

'You're right,' Robert replied.

'Of course,' Anna said, laughing. 'I usually am.'

Robert laughed too. 'Yeah, I should know that by now,' he said. 'The only thing I can impact is what comes next. I'm just going to use this disappointment to make me an even better player next season.'

'Bundesliga, watch out!' Anna said, reaching over to kiss him on the cheek.

## CHAPTER 18

# FALLING AT THE FINAL HURDLE

Every year that Robert spent with Jürgen and the Dortmund core, his standard of play rose to another level. Earlier in his career, he had gone into games hoping to score. Now he expected to score. With so many creative players around him, he had never been more excited to show up for preseason training.

'We've found a formula that works,' he told Anna at the start of the 2012–13 season. 'I really think this could be my best year yet.'

Heading into the final months of that season, his prediction was looking pretty good. Though Bayern were cruising to the Bundesliga title, Dortmund were in the hunt to finish second and Robert was in contention to be the league's top scorer. Even better, they had reached the Champions League semi-finals, where a huge test awaited.

'Can you believe we're playing Real Madrid?' Robert asked his mum when they spoke the week before the first leg. 'It's the kind of thing I probably dreamed up when I was a kid playing in the garden.'

'I stopped keeping count of your surreal football moments a long time ago,' Iwona replied, laughing. 'There have been so many achievements that eight-year-old Robert would never have believed possible.'

'You're right. But this one might be top of that list. That white Real shirt and all the history... and then playing at the Bernabéu in the second leg.'

Still, as much as he admired Real Madrid, there was no fear. By the time Dortmund walked onto the pitch for the first leg, fresh from a typically energetic Jürgen team talk, Robert and his teammates believed that they could match Real.

Robert was rarely the one shouting to pump up his teammates, but even he was buzzing in the tunnel. 'Let's go, boys. Let's go!' he called out, high-fiving

İlkay and throwing some pretend punches at Marco Reus, a newer member of the squad who had already served up many assists.

It only took six minutes for Robert to get a sight of goal, as Marco's shot was pushed out towards him. He couldn't squeeze in his follow-up effort, but the early signs were promising. He gave Marco a thumbs up. Two minutes later, Mario worked a crossing angle on the left and Robert instinctively peeled away to the back post. The cross was perfect and Robert watched it all the way, then guided it carefully into the bottom corner.

*Goooooooooooooooooooaaaaaaaaaaaaaaaaalllllllllllllll llllllllllll!!!!!!!!!!!!!!!!!!!!*

It was the dream start, and Robert could see the joy all over Jürgen's face.

Just before half-time, Marco surged into the penalty area again and fell in a tangle of legs. Robert raised his arms and turned to the referee, sure that Dortmund would have the chance to take a two-goal lead. Instead, the referee waved away the appeal, Real counter-attacked, and Cristiano Ronaldo equalised.

What had just happened? Robert rushed over to the referee to try to get answers.

At half-time, Jürgen was even more fired up than usual, but he also urged the team to play with controlled anger. 'Let that decision fuel your intensity, but keep your cool. Ending up with ten men on the pitch isn't going to help us.'

It took just four minutes for Robert to make Real pay. Marco struck a low shot from the edge of the box, but scuffed it on his weaker foot. Robert was the quickest to react, taking one touch to control the ball and a second to poke it into the net.

*Goooooooooooooooooooooaaaaaaaaaaaaaaaaalllllllllllllll llllllllllll!!!!!!!!!!!!!!!!!!!!!*

Now it was Real's turn to appeal to the officials, convinced that Robert had been offside. With Real heads still spinning, Robert struck a hammer blow. Again, the ball rolled free in the box. This time, he cushioned it, created half a yard with a clever drag back and thumped a shot into the top corner.

*Goooooooooooooooooooooaaaaaaaaaaaaaaaaalllllllllllllll llllllllllll!!!!!!!!!!!!!!!!!!!!!*

A hat-trick against Real Madrid. 'That's a stunner!' Marco yelled in his ear as they ran over to the Dortmund fans.

Real were on the ropes, and Robert knew it. 'Let's get another one, boys. Put the ball in the box.'

Marco burst forward yet again and was bundled to the ground. Penalty! And there was no question over who was taking it.

Robert placed the ball on the spot and made up his mind that, with the form he was in, he was going for power with this penalty. He waited for the whistle, then smashed the ball straight down the middle. The net rippled.

*Goooooooooooooooooooaaaaaaaaaaaaaaaaalllllllllllllll llllllllllll!!!!!!!!!!!!!!!!!!!!!*

Robert raised four fingers in the air as his teammates raced over to him. What a night!

At the final whistle, the Real players looked stunned as they shook hands. Robert understood why – he could hardly believe the past ninety minutes either.

'Are we going to wake up tomorrow and discover this was all just a dream?' İlkay asked, putting his arm round Robert. 'Four goals, big man. Incredible.'

Jürgen was on the pitch now too, savouring the moment with his players. 'Go over to the fans,' he told Robert and İlkay after wrapping them both in bear hugs.

The Dortmund players joined hands and ran over. Robert couldn't ever remember hearing the stadium as loud as it was tonight. Sitting on the pitch with his teammates all around him, the scoreline – and his performance – began to sink in.

'You just scored four goals against Real Madrid!' Anna said, screaming through the phone excitedly. 'This is crazy!'

Even with a three-goal cushion, the second leg brought a nail-biting finish. Real scored twice in the last ten minutes in a desperate late rally, but a 2–0 loss was enough to take Dortmund through to the final.

'I've never celebrated a loss this much before,' Robert joked as the players high-fived on the pitch.

'We're going to the Champions League final, boys!' Mario screamed, sparking more hugging and dancing.

The final would be against a familiar rival, Bayern

Munich, and the Dortmund players were well-aware that finishing as the runner-up to Bayern was in danger of becoming a trend. 'This is our day!' Jürgen said again and again in the dressing room. 'No fear, no regrets. You belong on this stage – believe it!'

Dortmund began on the front foot. Robert had one long range shot tipped over the bar and a close-range effort blocked. 'We're creating chances,' he said to Marco as they waited for a throw in. 'We just need to finish one.'

But as Robert watched from the other end of the pitch, Bayern made the breakthrough. Arjen Robben's cross gave Mario Mandžukic a tap-in. Some teams might have crumbled, but not Dortmund. With Jürgen barking instructions and willing his team to fight back, Marco won a penalty. This time, İlkay took the responsibility, slotting the spot-kick calmly into the bottom corner.

Just as the game seemed to be heading to extra time, Bayern broke Dortmund hearts. Franck Ribéry set up Robben, who skipped past two tackles and scuffed a low shot that trickled over the line. The scoreboard showed eighty-nine minutes. There was no time for a comeback. At the final whistle, Robert crouched down and stared at the ground. It was a cruel ending to a magical season.

Back in the dressing room, Jürgen let the players have their space. But after the tears had been wiped away and the shock had worn off, he wanted to get his message across. Robert finished taking off his socks and shinpads, still digesting the fact that Dortmund had fallen short again. He turned to face his manager.

'Boys, I could not be prouder of what you achieved tonight and this whole season,' Jürgen said. 'What a ride! There's no group of players I'd rather have by my side. It didn't go our way tonight, but when the pain wears off a little, I want you to remember this season as one of great success, not of near misses.'

Robert tried to keep those words in mind as he headed off for some overdue family time. There had been games that season that Dortmund fans would still be talking about in twenty years, and he was proud of what the team had achieved.

## CHAPTER 19

# BAYERN COME CALLING

The vibe around the Dortmund training ground felt different to Robert as he prepared for the start of the 2013–14 season. That was partly because he missed his friend, Mario, who had completed a dream move to Bayern over the summer. Without his sidekick, Robert would face even more responsibility.

But the other unsettling issue was that Robert's contract at Dortmund was due to expire at the end of the season. While the club was desperate to sign him to a long-term deal, Robert wanted to consider all of his options. It was no secret that Bayern were interested in him as the clinical finisher to link up with their midfield playmakers, and he knew that was a once-in-a-lifetime opportunity.

'Who wouldn't want to play for Bayern?' Robert told Cezary. 'But I love Dortmund, and Jürgen has been so good to me. I just... I just don't know what to do.'

He talked to Iwona and Milena and even called Mario to get the inside scoop on life at Bayern.

As the new season kicked off, Robert had to answer question after question about his future plans. 'I'm still deciding and there's a lot to think about,' he explained. 'For now, I'm a Dortmund player and we're getting ready to fight for the title again.'

But the speculation and attention were an unsettling distraction. As Dortmund struggled to keep pace with Bayern, Robert knew the decision day was looming.

'You'll have the option of signing a pre-contract agreement with another club in January,' Cezary reminded him.

During the Bundesliga winter break, Jürgen called Robert into his office. 'Lewy, if you've learned one thing about me over the years, I hope it's that I always want the best for my players, even if that means they move on.'

Robert paused, afraid to say the wrong thing.

'We'd love you to stay at Dortmund,' Jürgen replied. 'But I have a feeling your heart is telling you that you'll have regrets if you don't join Bayern. All I can say is that I'll respect your decision, whatever that is.'

Around the same time, Karl-Heinz Rummenigge was leading the charge to bring Robert to Bayern. 'With you leading the attack, we'll be unstoppable,' he told Robert. 'We're already a great team, but you can take us to an even higher level.'

By early January, Robert had made up his mind. He was going to Bayern.

In some ways, it felt good to have made the decision. No more rumours, no more questions. But he still felt bad for his teammates, many of whom had become good friends over the last few years. All he could do was try to finish the year on a high note.

Saying goodbye to the Dortmund fans after his final home game was even tougher than Robert had expected. He assumed that some of the crowd would still be angry about his decision to join Bayern, but he was overwhelmed to see the whole stadium applauding as the stadium announcer called out 'Thank you for four wonderful years!'

Fans waved their yellow-and-black scarves, and some were even in tears. Robert had to bite his lip to hold back tears of his own. 'I'm going to miss this place,' he said quietly to himself, then continued walking around the pitch waving to the fans.

'You arrived in Dortmund as a class striker and you're leaving as a *world* class striker,' Jürgen said, hugging Robert. 'I wish you all the best at Bayern… just not when you're playing us!'

**CHAPTER 20**

# NINE MAGICAL MINUTES

Robert was pleased with the way he had started life at Bayern. He was scoring goals, his chemistry with his teammates was getting better every week, and he was seeing the game even more vividly under Pep Guardiola's guidance. In his first season, Robert had scored twenty-five goals and Bayern had cruised to the title.

'What's been your highlight at Bayern so far, Lewy?' Mario asked him one summer afternoon as they sat outside in his back garden.

Robert paused and thought back through the last year. 'Well, winning the Bundesliga again was amazing,' he answered. 'The fans are great here too.'

'They definitely love you too!' Mario replied, laughing. 'But is there one game that stands out?'

There were a few possible answers – his Bayern debut, his first Champions League goal, the day they clinched the league – but Robert was surprised that this was such a difficult question. 'There have been some great moments, but I think the kind of Bayern highlight that I'll tell my kids about one day is still to come.'

Little did Robert know just how soon that day would come.

A few weeks later, Bayern took on Wolfsburg in a key early season clash, and Robert was initially frustrated to be on the bench as he shook off an ankle injury. 'Don't worry, you'll be involved tonight,' Pep explained. 'I just don't want to push it with a full ninety minutes.'

With Bayern trailing 1–0 at half-time, Pep walked over to Robert on his way to the dressing room, with a concerned look on his face. 'Get some stretches in during the break and be ready to come on,' he said. 'We'll make the change straightaway at the start of the second half.'

Excellent, Robert thought, as he dribbled a ball onto the pitch and got himself focused on turning the game around.

The crowd roared as Robert's name was announced on the stadium speakers. He high-fived Thomas Müller and Mario. 'Let's get back into this, lads!' he called out.

Bayern swarmed forward, with Robert darting into the box as Mario whipped in a cross. Arturo Vidal flicked it back to Thomas and, just as it looked like his touch was too heavy, Robert appeared out of nowhere to steer the ball into the net.

*Goooooooooooooooooooaaaaaaaaaaaaaaaaalllllllllllllll llllllllllllll!!!!!!!!!!!!!!!!!!!!*

Over on the touchline, Pep called out more instructions, then turned to his assistants. 'Six minutes and Lewy has already got us back in the game. He's a phenomenon!'

But Robert wasn't satisfied yet. He could sense the panic in the Wolfsburg defence with so many Bayern players capable of scoring. From the very next attack, he got the ball twenty-five yards out and only had one thought in his mind: drive on and hit it. Robert took one touch and the Wolfsburg defenders backed off further. He steadied himself and rocketed a low shot into the bottom corner. Unsaveable.

*Goooooooooooooooooooooaaaaaaaaaaaaaaaalllllllllllllll llllllllllll!!!!!!!!!!!!!!!!!!*

The crowd went wild. 'Are you kidding me?' Arturo said, running over to jump on Robert's back. 'What a strike!'

Now Wolfsburg were really rattled. Two minutes later, Bayern were in again. A long pass from Arturo sent Thomas through on goal. He laid it off to Mario as Robert screamed, 'Back post!' Mario clipped the ball across, and Robert hammered a shot against the post. The ball took a lucky bounce back to him and he managed to bundle it over the line.

*Goooooooooooooooooooooaaaaaaaaaaaaaaaalllllllllllllll llllllllllll!!!!!!!!!!!!!!!!!!*

Pep was all smiles on the touchline. Douglas Costa and Thomas were the first to wrap Robert in hugs. 'Unbelievable, big man,' Thomas said, shaking his head in amazement. 'You've crushed them.'

The fans were on their feet now every time Robert got the ball. Some strikers might have patted themselves on the back for scoring a hat-trick and taken it easy for the rest of the game, but not Robert. He wanted more. As Douglas burst away down the left, Robert sprinted into the box and called for the cutback. The cross sat up perfectly for him and he smashed a shot past the goalkeeper.

*Goooooooooooooooooooaaaaaaaaaaaaaaaaallllllllllllll llllllllllll!!!!!!!!!!!!!!!!!!!*

As he headed back to the halfway line, he was almost walking on air. On the way, he passed a few Wolfsburg players who looked completely stunned – and for a few seconds he felt bad for blowing their game plan apart. But Bayern were soon on the attack again and Robert sensed more chances were coming his way.

Mario looked up and floated a ball towards Robert just inside the penalty area. With his confidence as high as it had ever been, Robert did not even think about taking a touch to control it. He just swivelled and unleashed a first-time volley that flew into the top corner.

*Goooooooooooooooooooaaaaaaaaaaaaaaaaallllllllllllll llllllllllll!!!!!!!!!!!!!!!!!!!*

The whole Bayern team chased Robert over to the corner flag, with goalkeeper Manuel Neuer running the length of the pitch to join the celebrations. 'You can't miss!' Mario shouted. 'What a performance!'

'Yeah, but he's never going to stop talking about this!' Philipp Lahm added, laughing.

Pep stood with his hands over his face, grinning. 'I've never seen anything like this!' he told one of his assistants, who looked just as shocked as he was.

At the final whistle, Robert grabbed the match ball as players on both teams stopped to congratulate him. It was only back in the dressing room that he understood the records he had broken.

'Take your pick,' Pep said, reading from a list he had received from the Bayern media team. 'Fastest hat-trick in Bundesliga history, most goals scored by a substitute in the Bundesliga, first player to score five goals in a Bundesliga game since 1991 (and all within nine minutes!), first player to score five for Bayern since 1984...'

Mario and Arturo pretended to yawn. 'Okay, that's enough!' Thomas said, smiling. 'It's all going to go to his head, we might as well start calling him LewanGOALski!'

The players all gathered round to sign the match ball, and Robert made sure his shirt was put aside. He wanted to frame that and put it up at home.

As he and Mario walked out to the car park, Robert just shook his head. 'I still can't believe that just happened.'

'Well, you were saying you didn't have an unforgettable Bayern game yet,' Mario replied. 'I think you've got one now!'

Robert carried that form into the rest of the season, firing Bayern to another Bundesliga title and the DFB-Pokal cup. 'What a year, Lewy!' Pep said, hugging him on the pitch as they celebrated with the fans. 'If it wasn't clear already, this season proved you're the best striker in the world.'

## CHAPTER 21

# JOINING THE 100 CLUB

'It's a big day today!' Arturo said, patting Robert on the chest as he walked into the dressing room. 'Ninety-eight Bayern goals and counting. Could this be the day for number one hundred?'

Robert smiled. 'Depends how greedy you're feeling,' he joked.

It had been the big story all week, with Robert now on ninety-eight goals for the club in all competitions and reporters eager to know how he would celebrate his hundredth goal. In truth, he had nothing planned – but he knew that wasn't the answer they wanted.

'Well, I've got to get to one hundred first, then I'll worry about the celebration,' he had said countless times over the last few days.

It had been another typical Bayern season so far. Carlo Ancelotti had replaced Pep as manager, but little else had changed. Robert was still banging in goals and the rest of the league struggled to keep pace.

As he stepped onto the pitch with his teammates to face Eintracht Frankfurt, he took a minute to look around the Allianz Arena that had become a second home over the past few years. The sea of red shirts were already singing and chanting, ready for another show from Robert, Arjen and co.

But the Frankfurt defence were not going to make it easy for Robert to join Bayern's exclusive one-hundred goal club, with tight man-marking and a swarm of extra tacklers any time he tried to turn. Then his flick header bounced nicely for Thomas, who took one touch to create an extra yard for a cross. Robert knew what to expect. While his marker moved to deny him a cutback, Robert instead darted for a square pass across the face of the goal. They had worked on that so many times in training that he didn't even have to call for it. Thomas whipped in the cross and Robert had the simple job of tapping the ball into an empty net.

*Goooooooooooooooooooaaaaaaaaaaaaaaaallllllllllllll llllllllllll!!!!!!!!!!!!!!!!!!!*

Number ninety-nine! Robert pointed to Thomas to recognise the perfect pass. 'Here we go!' Arturo shouted. 'One more to go!'

The crowd could sense it too, as the volume was cranked up every time he got the ball within shooting distance.

As Philipp clipped a pass down the right wing to Arjen, Robert was still well outside the box. But, knowing Arjen liked to cut inside, he still had time. Robert sprinted into the area whilst waving his arm up. 'Arjen, back post!' he called.

Arjen created an angle for the cross and dinked the ball into the box. It went just over Thomas's head but Robert swivelled, took a chance and drilled a shot into the net before the goalkeeper could even dive.

*Goooooooooooooooooooaaaaaaaaaaaaaaaallllllllllllll llllllllllll!!!!!!!!!!!!!!!!!!!*

Robert raised both arms to take the applause from the fans. Thomas and Arjen raced over to high-five him. 'That's one hundred, big man!' Arjen shouted. 'You can thank me later for the assist.'

Robert laughed. 'Nice try. I know you were aiming for Thomas!'

Back in the dressing room, Carlo gathered the team to present Robert with the match ball – another souvenir to add to his collection. 'Scoring one hundred goals for one club is an incredible achievement and you've done it in just 137 games, which is just remarkable,' Carlo said, as the rest of the dressing room cheered loudly.

Captain Philipp Lahm picked up Robert's Number 9 shirt while Robert showered and got the whole team to write messages. 'Nice messages, please,' Philippe said, looking at Arturo, who burst out laughing.

When Robert saw all the messages, he had to take a deep breath so he didn't cry. 'This is amazing, lads. Thank you! I love being part of this team. I'm only standing here with one hundred Bayern goals because you keep creating the chances for me – even Arjen passes to me sometimes!' Arjen nodded his head, laughing.

Bayern powered on to yet another title, but the Champions League again eluded Robert. 'That's the one I really want now,' he told Anna as they relaxed at home.

Anna looked up and put her finger over her mouth. 'Shhhh!' Anna whispered. 'She's sleeping.'

Robert mouthed 'sorry' and walked over to his wife, who was holding their daughter, Klara, who was just two months old. She was waking up.

Anna passed Klara to Robert, who scooped her up carefully and looked down at her beautiful little face.

'You've got plenty of years to chase that trophy,' Anna said, smiling a sneaky smile. 'In the meantime, you can change that nappy!'

## CHAPTER 22

# EURO REDEMPTION

As the Poland squad worked through a range of training drills before Euro 2016, no-one needed to remind Robert about the need to make amends for their group stage exit four years earlier. He still had painful memories of sitting on the pitch after the final group game and the silent dressing room afterwards, but now he and his teammates had a fresh opportunity to make the Polish fans proud. After wrapping up yet another Bundesliga title with Bayern, Robert was full of confidence.

'At Euro 2012, we were the hosts and our fans had high expectations,' he told Anna as he was packing his suitcase for the tournament. 'This time, it's different. We didn't qualify for the last World Cup so just making it to Euro 2016 was a big step. Now that we're here, I think we're going to surprise people.'

It was a different group of players too. Although there were some familiar faces from the Euro 2012 squad, there were also a handful of new call-ups. The draw had placed Poland in Group C with Germany, Northern Ireland and Ukraine, and Robert had received plenty of texts from his German teammates. 'We'll try to go easy on you guys,' Manuel Neuer joked.

First, Poland needed to get a result against Northern Ireland. As Robert stood at the front of the Polish line in the tunnel, he fiddled with his captain's armband and rolled his neck from side to side. Leading the team out at a big tournament like this was an incredible feeling. The referee gave the signal and Robert took a deep breath. He could already hear the Poland fans making plenty of noise.

Through the anthems and the coin toss, he felt his whole body tingling – part nerves, part excitement. Mostly excitement. It was clear that Northern Ireland's game plan centred around giving Robert no space, and he often saw two defenders shadowing him. But he kept it simple, laying the ball off and letting his teammates exploit the extra space. When Arkadiusz Milik fired in the only goal of the game, Robert was sprinting towards the goal in case of a rebound. He raised his arms in the air as he saw the ball fly into the net and turned to join the celebrations on the touchline.

'It makes such a difference to be heading into the Germany game with three points on the board,' Robert told Iwona when she called to get his verdict on the game. 'We can play better than we did in the first game, though, and we'll need to against Germany – otherwise life at Bayern will be pretty tough!'

Despite some good chances at both ends, Poland and Germany had to settle for a 0–0 draw. 'We're right where we want to be,' Poland's manager Adam Nawałka said after the game. Robert felt the same way, though he was desperate for some decent chances after two quiet games.

Jakub was the hero in the final group game, sending Poland through to the knockout rounds with a second-half winner. Robert led the players over to the Polish fans at the end of the game, relishing the chance to have the kind of special moment that he had hoped for back at Euro 2012. 'We did it!' Robert shouted to Jakub, who could barely hear with all the cheering. 'This is the furthest a Polish team has ever gone at the Euros!'

Switzerland stood between Robert and a trip to the quarter-finals. While Adam was having to answer some questions in press conferences about why his star striker hadn't scored yet at the tournament, Robert did not let it affect him. The team was winning – that was all that mattered.

And when a penalty shootout was needed against Switzerland after a 1–1 draw, Robert didn't hesitate to put his hand up for one of the spot-kicks. 'I'll go first,' he said. He had been hitting his penalties well in training and wanted the responsibility of getting the team off to a good start.

Robert placed the ball on the spot, took six paces backwards and paused for a moment to compose himself. Then he jogged up and smashed

an unstoppable penalty just inside the post. The
goalkeeper dived the right way, but had no chance.

When Switzerland missed their second penalty, the
Poland huddle on the halfway line became even more
on edge. The players had their arms linked together,
and Robert felt like his heart was going to pop out of
his chest. Their first four penalties found the net and
it was left to Grzegorz Krychowiak to walk up for the
fifth one. Robert could hardly breathe with all the
tension. He wanted to close his eyes, but he forced
himself to watch.

Grzegorz hammered his penalty into the top corner,
and Poland were through. 'Wooooooooooooooo!' Robert
screamed, sprinting over with all his teammates. What
a moment!

Robert replayed that shootout again and again as
he lay in bed that night. He was so proud of his team
and their clinical penalties. But now he needed his
rest, because five days later they would face Cristiano
Ronaldo and Portugal in the quarter-finals.

It had been a team effort to get this far, but Robert
knew that the latter stages of tournaments was when

star players really made their names and he desperately wanted a goal. As the Poland fans sang his name during the warm-up, he felt even more locked in.

Inside the first two minutes, a Portugal mistake let the ball reach Kamil Grosicki on the left. Robert knew what to expect. Kamil took two touches and drove in a skidding cross. Robert timed his run perfectly, getting to the ball ahead of his marker and sending a first-time shot into the bottom corner.

*Gooooooooooooooooooooaaaaaaaaaaaaaaaaalllllllllllllll lllllllllllll!!!!!!!!!!!!!!!!!!!*

Finally! 'Yes!' Robert screamed, as Jakub jumped on his back.

But once Portugal equalised, Poland were hanging on. 'Keep fighting!' Robert urged his defenders, who were having to throw their bodies in the way of relentless attacks. Fortunately, Poland hung on for another penalty shootout.

'We've been here before, lads,' Robert said, clapping his hands to rally his weary teammates. 'Take your time and pick your spot.'

Again, Robert would go first for Poland. He picked

up the ball, bounced it a few times and settled himself down. In the shootout against Switzerland, he had gone for power. This time, he waited for the goalkeeper to dive to the left, and calmly stroked the ball into the opposite corner. Robert looked towards the Poland fans and pumped his fist.

But Portugal did not look like missing, as penalty after penalty flew into the net. Jakub stepped up for Poland's fourth penalty as Robert felt his legs shaking on the halfway line. The penalty was well hit but brilliantly saved. Robert felt like he'd been punched in the stomach. As Portugal scored the winning penalty, Robert put his hands on his knees. This really stung.

He walked over to Jakub and put his arm around him. 'Don't blame yourself, buddy,' he said softly. 'These shootouts are a lottery and that was a good penalty.'

No-one said much in the dressing room afterwards. Tired bodies were slumped at their stalls and tired minds tried to digest how close they had been to the semi-finals. Eventually, Robert stood up and addressed the team. 'This one hurts and it's going to hurt for a while, but I couldn't be prouder to walk onto the pitch with you guys. We've made people all over Poland really proud over the last few weeks and, once enough time passes, we're going to remember this bond we formed and the memories we created.'

Some of his teammates were in tears, and he went to hug each of them.

'I couldn't have said it any better than Robert just did,' manager Adam added. 'This has been a magical few weeks and you've achieved something that no Poland team has ever managed to do. Keep your heads up and focus on the positives from this tournament.'

As Robert set off for a few weeks away with Anna and Klara, he knew he needed this break. Another big season was just around the corners and, as always, the expectations at Bayern would be sky high.

## CHAPTER 23

# THE MISSING PIECE

'I hope you're building a bigger trophy room,' Milena joked as they walked through a park near her house before the start of the 2018–19 season. 'You started off needing a couple of shelves, and now even that room in the basement isn't big enough.'

Robert smiled. He'd been thinking the same thing lately, in part to take his mind off Poland's disappointing 2018 World Cup performance. His Bayern career had been a whirlwind of goals and trophies so far.

'By my count, you've got four Bundesliga titles with Bayern, plus the two at Dortmund, then two DFB-Pokal cups and two DFL-Supercups.'

'Something like that,' Robert replied, pretending to have lost count. 'I think you forgot my three Bundesliga top scorer awards, but that's okay.'

They both giggled.

'But I still want more,' Robert said. 'Most of all, I want to win the Champions League. That's the one I need to complete my set.'

Even as some of the Bayern legends hung up their boots or moved on to other clubs, the club continued to uncover superstars to take their places. As Robert looked around the cafeteria early in the season, he was stunned to notice that he was now one of the senior Bayern leaders. Youngsters like Joshua Kimmich and Serge Gnabry were ready for bigger roles, and he knew that the next wave of academy talents would soon be knocking on the first team door.

With rumours floating around linking Real Madrid with a move for Robert, he just kept his focus on what he did best: scoring goals. A ruthless Super Cup hat-trick was his latest reminder that there wasn't a better finisher in world football.

He saved some of his best performances for the

Champions League. As the competition's top scorer during the group stage, he was leading the way for his teammates. 'This is our year!' he kept saying as Bayern powered to the top of Group E.

Robert knew their tie with Liverpool in the next round would be tougher, but the mood in the dressing room was upbeat after a 0–0 draw at Anfield in the first leg. 'I'd fancy our chances of beating anyone at home,' Robert said to Joshua as they got back on the team bus to return to the hotel. 'And that's all we'll need to do.'

But it all went wrong in the second leg, as Liverpool stunned the Allianz Arena with a 3–1 win. At 1–1, Robert had felt sure that Bayern would find the breakthrough, but a poor second half had derailed them at the worst possible moment – and they all had to take a share of the blame.

Bayern wrapped up another Bundesliga title – Robert's fifth in a row – but their early Champions League exit still haunted Robert as he watched Liverpool go on to lift the trophy. 'Maybe it's just not meant to be,' he told his mum that summer as they talked about his future plans. 'I'm going to be thirty-two next year and I'm running out of chances to add "Champions League winner" to my CV.'

Iwona smiled at her son's never-ending ambition. 'Keep believing,' she said. 'At a club like Bayern, you'll always have a chance and, what is it they say?' She paused, then remembered. 'Ah yes – all good things come to those who wait!'

## CHAPTER 24

# KINGS OF
# EUROPE

As Robert put on his Number 9 shirt and laced his
boots, his pre-game routine was about the only normal
thing in a completely unusual 2019–20 season. With
health concerns across Germany and around the world,
the Bundesliga and Champions League had been
paused, then restarted without any fans in the stadiums.

In ten minutes, Bayern would be taking on
Barcelona in a Champions League quarter-final.
Normally, he would be able to hear the fans and feel
the stadium rocking. Instead, they were playing at a
neutral venue in Portugal with no-one in the stands.

'Look on the bright side,' Serge said. 'At least they'll
be no-one to boo you if you miss a sitter!'

'Thanks, buddy,' Robert replied, laughing.

By now, the Bayern players were used to this new crowd-less reality, having played plenty of Bundesliga games without fans. Hansi Flick, the latest manager leading the Bayern trophy charge, had insisted that they approach games exactly as they typically would, ignoring the circumstances and maintaining their usual routines.

Fans or no fans, there was always something special about facing Lionel Messi. Robert always enjoyed talking with him at the awards nights, but tonight Lionel and Barcelona were the enemy.

'Let's get after it early on, lads,' Thomas yelled after the Champions League anthem, his voice echoing around the empty stadium.

Robert did five quick sprints to make sure he was sharp right from the first whistle. For all Barcelona's fine attacking play, he knew they could be caught out defensively and wanted to be ready when the chances came.

Within five minutes, Thomas had taken his own advice. Ivan Perišić got free on the left and floated a cross to the edge of the box. Robert had made a different run, but it fell perfectly for Thomas. Robert turned just as his teammate flicked the ball towards him and he played the one-two with a cushioned touch of his left foot. Thomas ran onto the pass and smashed a shot into the bottom corner. What a start!

When David Alaba sliced the ball into his own net minutes later, Robert didn't even hold his head in disappointment. He had seen enough in the first few minutes to know that Bayern were going to get a hatful of chances at the other end. Barcelona were leaving all kinds of space out wide and their defenders looked completely lost whenever Robert and the midfielders put them under pressure. Robert looked over to the touchline and saw Hansi clapping. 'Keep pressing!'

Bayern went back in front from another Barcelona giveaway. Ivan fired in a shot off the bar, with Robert sliding in just in case it bounced out. Minutes later, Serge got behind the defence and tucked away his chance. 3–1.

Robert kept hounding the Barcelona back line and almost grabbed a fourth goal for Bayern after winning a tackle near the edge of the box. He stared in shock as the goalkeeper got a toe to his shot and sent it wide of the post. Soon after Robert was celebrating again as Thomas was quickest to Joshua's cross and poked the ball home. It was 4–1 and there were still fourteen minutes until half-time.

Even the most optimistic Bayern fan couldn't have predicted this thumping scoreline – and they weren't finished yet. Barcelona pulled a goal back, but their momentum didn't last long. Alphonso Davies, Bayern's new teenage Canadian prodigy, danced clear on the left, raced to the by-line and took his time. Robert's near post run distracted three Barcelona defenders, and Alphonso cut the ball back for Joshua to drill home. Five goals in just over an hour!

Robert couldn't remember being part of a better Bayern performance than this. But he still wanted his goal. Thankfully, his teammates were still sprinting forward to create more chances. Coutinho tricked his way clear on the left and floated the ball to the back post. Robert's eyes lit up as he climbed to power in a free header.

*Goooooooooooooooooooooaaaaaaaaaaaaaaaalllllllllllllll llllllllllllll!!!!!!!!!!!!!!!!!!!!*

Finally!

Two late goals from Coutinho completed an 8–2 masterclass for Bayern. The Barcelona players looked completely stunned as they walked off at the final whistle. Arturo, now playing for Barcelona, just shrugged when Robert walked over for a high-five. 'We couldn't get near you guys,' Arturo said.

'If it's any consolation, I think that's one of the best games we've ever played,' Robert replied, trying to show some sympathy for his friend.

'Well that really makes me feel better!' Arturo fired back, sarcastically. They both laughed.

The Bayern dressing room was loud and excited for the first time in this strange stop-start season. But Robert was quick to remind his teammates of the mission they were on. 'Let's enjoy this tonight, boys, but there's still hard work ahead if we want to end our Champions League drought. We still need two more wins.'

Manuel appeared next to Robert, putting his arm

round his neck. 'He's right, and this performance should give us all the confidence we need. We were clinical tonight – even you, David!'

They all laughed as Manuel did an impression of David's spectacular own goal, and even David was on the floor giggling.

With the Bundesliga title race swinging in Bayern's favour, they could afford to throw their energy into their Champions League semi-final against Lyon. But Robert watched from the other end of the pitch nervously as Lyon created two great early chances and wasted both.

'Come on, boys,' he shouted. 'Switch on!'

Serge then made Lyon pay, scoring a screamer from outside the box then tapping in a simple chance after Robert somehow missed an open net. 'Thanks, Serge,' Robert said, laughing. 'Hopefully now people will forget about my miss.'

As Lyon launched a desperate late rally, Robert sensed a chance to strike on the counter-attack. When Joshua swung in a free kick, Robert leapt just like he'd learned in his volleyball days. He got to the ball first and headed it down into the bottom corner. A textbook header.

*Goooooooooooooooooooaaaaaaaaaaaaaaaaalllllllllllllll llllllllllll!!!!!!!!!!!!!!!!!!!!!*

That sealed it. Bayern were into the Champions League final. Exhausted, Robert crouched down at the final whistle and tapped the ground in a mix of celebration and relief. He would finally have another chance to lift this elusive trophy!

With the unique format of this season's Champions League, Robert was grateful that he only had to wait a few days for the final. Still, he could hardly sleep. The 2013 final felt like forever ago, but he still remembered the heartbreak of sitting on the pitch after losing that night. He couldn't let another Champions League slip through his fingers. Paris St Germain stood in Bayern's way – and Robert knew that Kylian Mbappé and Neymar could change the game in a flash.

On the day of the final, Robert did his best to treat it like any another game. But the Bayern dressing room was a little quieter than normal as the players battled the nerves. 'Stay loose,' Hansi said, but even he was pacing the room. 'We've got this far by playing our football and you deserve a ton of credit for battling through all the challenges this year. Now let's go and win this trophy.'

As Robert walked down the tunnel, he caught sight of the Champions League trophy at the edge of the pitch. He was already fired up, but seeing the trophy there just took it to another level. 'What a beauty!' he said under his breath.

Robert was soon in the thick of the action. Minutes after Manuel had made a key save to deny Neymar, a cross for Alphonso bounced through a crowded penalty area. Robert pounced on it, taking one touch to create an angle and another to fire a shot across the goalkeeper. He watched in agony as it came back off the post. Later in the first half, he reacted sharply to get a header on target, but it was straight at the keeper. Though he tapped his thigh in frustration, he could feel a goal coming.

And it did just before the hour mark. Joshua swung the ball in from the right and Robert back-pedalled,

desperately trying to reach it. Then he heard the
call from winger Kingsley Coman, who swooped in
to direct a header into the bottom corner. Bayern
were ahead!

Robert watched the minutes tick by. Every minute
felt like an hour. Ten minutes to go. Five minutes to
go. Into stoppage time. He kept chasing every hoofed
clearance, determined to give everything he had.
Finally, the referee blew his whistle. Bayern had won
the Champions League!

Robert fell to his knees and curled up into a ball,
with his head pressed into the pitch. The emotions
were too much for him and he needed this minute
alone before he could join in the party with his
teammates. He had thought about this moment so
many times, and now he would get his hands on the
trophy. He knew his family would be watching as well
as lots of friends in Poland and Germany. And Anna
and Klara of course, back at home with baby Laura,
the newest addition to the Lewandowski family. He
couldn't wait to hug them all.

Then he rushed over to the centre circle. He high-fived Serge and Alphonso, then hugged Manuel, who he had played alongside in so many big games over the years. They all knew that they would be bonded together forever by this win.

As he waited for his teammates to come up one by one and join him on the special podium, Robert looked in admiration at the Champions League winner's medal around his neck – the medal he had been chasing for so long. Then Manuel carried the trophy over and they all gathered around him. On the count of three, he raised it high into the air.

The perfect season came to an end with more trophies than Robert ever thought possible, capped off by the FIFA Men's Player of the Year award. 'I've got to capture this moment,' he told Anna one day, deep in thought. He made a few calls and managed to set up a day where he could have all the trophies – his individual ones and the ones he won with Bayern – at his house for a few hours.

Passing his phone to Anna, he lay down on the bed, surrounded by all the trophies. She laughed and took the photo. As he looked at the photo, he couldn't help but grin. It had been an incredible journey – and there were likely a few chapters still to be written. Robert put his arm around Anna and reflected once again on how lucky he was. 'Life doesn't get any better than this!' he said, smiling.

Read on for a sneak preview of
another brilliant football story by
Matt and Tom Oldfield. . .

SON

Available now!

**CHAPTER 1**

# A SONSATIONAL GOAL!

*7 December 2019, Tottenham Hotspur Stadium*

As Son Heung-min controlled the ball on the edge of his own box, he could already hear his teammates calling out to him. The counter-attack was on.

'Yes!' yelled Dele Alli, making a run to his left.

'Over here!' shouted Lucas Moura, unmarked in the middle.

But while Son Heung-min paused for a moment, thinking of the best pass to play, the Burnley defenders backed away and a space opened up right in front of him. So he kept going.

Why not? After all, Tottenham were already

winning 2–0, thanks to goals from Harry Kane and Lucas. Son Heung-min had set up the first for Harry, and now he wanted to score one of his own. He loved to dribble with the ball and a wondergoal would be the perfect way to impress his new manager, José Mourinho, especially after Spurs' disappointing defeat against Manchester United.

*ZOOM!* With a burst of speed, Son Heung-min carried the ball forward, leaving two Burnley players trailing behind. But now, he was dribbling straight towards two more defenders, and there was another one approaching from the right...

What next? Was it time to pass? No, Son Heung-min kept going. With two perfectly timed touches, he escaped past one player and then another. All of a sudden, to his great surprise, he was beyond the last Burnley defender and flying towards goal...

'Go on, Sonny!' the Tottenham supporters shouted as their excitement grew. 'Go on – what a goal this would be!'

Dele and Lucas were still racing forward in support, but Harry and Moussa Sissoko had both slowed down

to watch Son Heung-min's spectacular solo run. They
knew that their teammate had the speed and skill
to go all the way and score, as he had done so many
times in training. But to do it in a proper Premier
League match was a different matter...

'Go on, Sonny!'

As he entered the penalty area, Son Heung-min
slowed down to steady himself. And, he was starting
to feel really tired after his seventy-yard sprint! But
there was no way that he was going to rush his shot
and waste this chance, not after running all the way
from his own box. He was focused on finishing what
he'd started. So, he waited for the Burnley keeper to
dive and then coolly slotted the ball past him and into
the back of the net. *3–0!*

*Goooooooooooooooooooooaaaaaaaaaaaaaaaalllllllllllllll
lllllllllllll!!!!!!!!!!!!!!!!!!!*

As the Tottenham fans went wild all around him,
Son Heung-min jogged over to the corner flag with
his arms out wide and a big smile on his face. He felt
so happy and so proud – what a magical moment!
He had scored a lot of good goals in his career – for

Hamburg, Bayer Leverkusen, Tottenham and South Korea – but never one quite like this. For a few seconds, Son Heung-min just stood there, taking it all in – the atmosphere, the achievement. Then he nodded his head at the crowd; they had just witnessed something truly special and chanted:

*Nice one, Sonny, nice one Son,*
*Nice one, Sonny, let's have another one!*

'Well done, Sonny, but why didn't you pass it to me?!' Dele joked when he finally caught up with his friend. Harry was the next to arrive and he too hugged his teammate tightly. Lucas, meanwhile, just clapped and clapped like the 58,000 fans in the crowd. What else could you do after watching a wondergoal like that!

At the final whistle, it was Tottenham 5 Burnley 0, but there was only one goal that everyone was talking about.

'Wow,' Gary Lineker tweeted. 'Son has just scored one of the greatest individual goals you're ever likely to see.'

And England legend Alan Shearer agreed. 'It will

be getting goal of the season, won't it?' he predicted on *Match of the Day*. 'They might as well shut the competition now.' He was right about that, and after winning the Premier League award, Son Heung-min's wondergoal would go on to win the 2020 FIFA Puskás Award, a prestigious award given for the best goal scored across the whole world!

However, when he spoke to the media just minutes after scoring that beauty against Burnley, Son Heung-min was as modest as ever. 'It was really important for us to get three points again,' he said, before thanking his Tottenham teammates, his manager, and the club's supporters. 'I'm just really grateful.'

Although Son Heung-min was an amazing attacker who could score great goals, it was his winning personality that made the Premier League fall in love with him – his humble attitude, his remarkable work-rate, all the smiles and all the handshakes. That's what made the South Korean such a special superstar, and as with so many things in his life, he had his father to thank for that.

**Znicz Pruszków**

🏆 Polish Third Division: 2006–07

**Lech Poznań**

🏆 Ekstraklasa (Polish First Division): 2009–10

🏆 Polish Cup: 2008–09

🏆 Polish SuperCup: 2009

**Borussia Dortmund**

🏆 Bundesliga: 2010–11, 2011–12

🏆 DFB-Pokal: 2011–12

🏆 DFL-Supercup: 2013

## Bayern Munich

🏆 Bundesliga: 2014–15, 2015–16, 2016–17, 2017–18, 2018–19, 2019–20

🏆 DFB-Pokal: 2015–16, 2018–19, 2019–20

🏆 DFL-Supercup: 2016, 2017, 2018, 2020

🏆 UEFA Champions League: 2019–20

🏆 UEFA Super Cup: 2020

🏆 FIFA Club World Cup: 2020

## Individual

🏆 Polish Young Player of the Year: 2008

🏆 Ekstraklasa Best Player: 2009

🏆 Ekstraklasa top goalscorer: 2009–10

🏆 Polish Footballer of the Year: 2011, 2012, 2013, 2014, 2015, 2016, 2017, 2019, 2020

🏆 Bundesliga top goalscorer: 2013–14, 2015–16, 2017–18, 2018–19, 2019–20

🏆 UEFA Euro qualifying top goalscorer: 2016

🏆 Bundesliga Player of the Season: 2016–17, 2019–20

🏆 FIFA World Cup qualification top goalscorer: 2018

- 🏆 Bayern Munich Player of the Season: 2019–20
- 🏆 UEFA Men's Player of the Year: 2019–20
- 🏆 UEFA Champions League top goalscorer: 2019–20
- 🏆 UEFA Champions League top assist provider: 2019–20
- 🏆 The Best FIFA Men's Player: 2020

# LEWANDOWSKI

## 9 THE FACTS

**NAME:**
Robert Lewandowski

**DATE OF BIRTH:**
21 August 1988

**AGE:** 32

**PLACE OF BIRTH:**
Warsaw

**NATIONALITY:** Poland

**BEST FRIEND:** Mario Götze

**CURRENT CLUB:** Bayern Munich

**POSITION:** ST

## THE STATS

| | |
|---|---|
| Height (cm): | 185 |
| Club appearances: | 690 |
| Club goals: | 474 |
| Club trophies: | 24 |
| International appearances: | 116 |
| International goals: | 63 |
| International trophies: | 0 |
| Ballon d'Ors: | 0 |

★ ★ ★ **HERO RATING: 91** ★ ★ ★

# GREATEST MOMENTS

## 1  15 MAY 2010, LECH POZNAŃ 2–0 ZAGŁĘBIE LUBIN

Robert capped off a sensational second season in
the Ekstraklasa by scoring the crucial second goal
in this game, which confirmed his club, Lech Poznan
´, as the new Champions of Poland. Robert had played
a key part in his team's success, with eighteen goals
that season, and he was now one of Europe's hottest
strikers. A few months later, he made the move to
Germany to join Borussia Dortmund.

## 12 MAY 2012, BORUSSIA DORTMUND 5–2 BAYERN MUNICH

It took Robert a season to settle in German football, but after that he was unstoppable. The 2011–12 season was an incredible campaign for him and his teammates as Dortmund won the League and Cup double. For Robert, the highlight was undoubtedly this hat-trick in the German Cup final against their biggest rivals, Bayern.

## 24 APRIL 2013, BORUSSIA DORTMUND 4–1 REAL MADRID

After winning back-to-back Bundesliga titles, Robert and his Dortmund teammates took on their next challenge: the Champions League. After making it through to the semi-finals, they then thrashed Cristiano Ronaldo's Real Madrid in style, with Robert scoring all four goals. Unfortunately, Dortmund lost in the final to Bayern, who would soon steal their star striker too...

## 22 SEPTEMBER 2015, BAYERN MUNICH 5–1 WOLFSBURG

From the moment Robert arrived at Bayern Munich, he became their star striker and top scorer, taking his game to the next level. In this Bundesliga match, manager Pep Guardiola only brought him on at half-time and ten minutes later, he already had a hat-trick! In total, he scored five goals in just nine magical minutes.

## 23 AUGUST 2020, PARIS ST GERMAIN 0–1 BAYERN MUNICH

This was the unforgettable night when Robert finally added the last missing piece to his incredible trophy cabinet: the Champions League. Although he didn't manage to score in the final against PSG, his team won the match and that was all that mattered. Plus, Robert had already scored a whopping fifteen goals on the way to the final!

# PLAY LIKE YOUR HEROES

## THE ROBERT LEWANDOWSKI LEAP AND HEAD

Don't worry, you don't need to be ten foot tall to be brilliant in the air. Lewandowski is no giant, so instead he uses his intelligence, timing, and technique, like this:

**STEP 1:** As your teammates attack down the wings, get yourself into the box and stay alert for any crosses that arrive.

**STEP 2:** While you wait for the ball, think carefully and cleverly about where you should be. Which of the opposition defenders is the smallest, or the weakest in the air? If you can, get close to them, or sneak in between the centre-backs.

**STEP 3:** As soon as you see your teammate look up and pull their leg back for the cross, react fast and react first. Leap up high above your marker, but make sure you time your jump so that your head meets the ball at exactly the right moment.

**STEP 4:** Star strikers like Lewandowski always know where the goal is and where the goalkeeper is. If you're at the front post, go for a glancing header, flicking the ball off your head at an angle so that it flies towards the goal.

**STEP 5:** If you're in the middle or at the back post, it's often best to go for power, but don't forget to keep your header under control! And try to aim low towards one of the bottom corners to make it harder for the keeper to save.

**STEP 6:** GOAL! Celebrate by raising one arm up in the air like all star strikers and then rush over to thank your teammate for the amazing assist.

# TEST YOUR KNOWLEDGE

## QUESTIONS

**1.** What three sports did Robert's parents play when they were younger?

**2.** Which shirt number did Robert choose to wear for his first local youth team, Partyzant Leszno? (Clue: he still wears it now!)

**3.** Which English Premier League club did Robert choose to support as a boy and why?

**4.** As a youngster, Robert scored lots of goals, but what was the one thing that the scouts worried about?

**5.** Robert scored on his senior international debut for Poland – true or false?

6.  Who was the Borussia Dortmund manager when Robert signed for the club in 2010?

7.  In 2014, Robert moved from Borussia Dortmund to Bayern Munich, following in the footsteps of which friend and former teammate?

8.  How long did it take Robert to score five goals in a game against Wolfsburg in 2015?

9.  How many times did Robert score for Poland at Euro 2016?

10. Who scored the winning goal for Bayern Munich in the 2020 Champions League Final? (Clue: it wasn't Robert!)

11. Which two football legends did Robert beat to win the 2020 FIFA Men's Player of the Year award?

1. *Volleyball, judo, and football.* 2. *Number 9!* 3. *Arsenal – because he was a huge fan of their French striker, Thierry Henry.* 4. *They thought he was too skinny to be a top striker.* 5. *True – he had only been on the pitch for eight minutes when he scored against San Marino!* 6. *Jürgen Klopp* 7. *Mario Götze.* 8. *Nine minutes!* 9. *Three (one goal against Portugal, plus two spot-kicks in penalty shootouts)* 10. *Kingsley Coman.* 11. *Ronaldo and Messi!*

## CAN'T GET ENOUGH OF ULTIMATE FOOTBALL HEROES?

**Check out heroesfootball.com
for quizzes, games, and competitions!**

**Plus join the Ultimate Football Heroes
Fan Club to score exclusive content
and be the first to hear about new
books and events.
heroesfootball.com/subscribe/**